"In over 20 years of working with international students I haven't seen a book that is so tailored to their needs. Studying overseas is challenging but ultimately rewarding. This guide is an A to Z of how to study, work and live abroad successfully. It should be mandatory reading for all international students."

– **Jane Barrett**, *co-author of* Taking Charge of Your Career

"As a university professor who has both studied and taught in several different countries, I strongly recommend *The Essential Guide to Studying Abroad*, which does exactly what its title promises. Clearly written and accessible, the book features precious insight on how to apply successfully to international programs, adjust to life in a foreign land, ace tests and exams and, finally, get ready for the job market and prepare a winning résumé. A must-read for current and potential international students from all over the world."

– **Daniel Béland**, *Professor, Department of Political Science, McGill University, Montreal, Canada*

"*The Essential Guide to Studying Abroad* is an amazing book that answers just about every possible question you might have about studying overseas. It is the 'Lonely Planet' for the journey of international students. The book gives practical information for the entire student journey including the step into the job market."

– **Jelda Veninga**, *Senior Career Consultant, TIAS School for Business and Society, Netherlands*

"As a former international student myself and now an international educator who cares deeply about the internationalization of academia, I highly recommend the book. This is an invaluable manual for international students and a valuable resource for anyone interested in the success of young people studying abroad."

– **Naim Kapucu**, *Professor and Director, School of Public Administration, University of Central Florida, USA*

D1220759

The Essential Guide to Studying Abroad

This book is an indispensable how-to guide on flourishing when studying abroad, and how to use an international education to begin a fulfilling career after graduation.

Written in an engaging and accessible style, using many examples, case studies, and links to resources, the book reduces the stress of studying abroad. Covering all aspects of the international student experience – inside and outside the classroom – the book encourages young people to perform their very best and succeed in their new environment.

International students preparing for cross-cultural learning and recent graduates looking for employment will find this book both practical and inspiring.

Thomas R. Klassen is a Professor at York University in Toronto, Canada. He has taught in a variety of programmes, including the IMBA at the Schulich School of Business, the Department of Political Science, the School of Public Policy and Administration, and the Faculty of Health. He has taught university courses in South Korea (at Yonsei University) and Germany (at the University of Konstanz). He divides his time between Toronto, Canada, and Seoul, South Korea.

Christine Menges is Director of the Career Center, MBA Programs, at the WHU – Otto Beisheim School of Management, one of Germany's top business schools according to major national and international rankings. She has crafted WHU's career counselling approach and placement strategy for students with work experience, and forges networks with industry leaders. She holds a PhD in management with a special focus on mentoring from the University of St. Gallen in Switzerland.

The Essential Guide to Studying Abroad

From Success in the Classroom to a Fulfilling Career

Thomas R. Klassen and Christine Menges

Routledge
Taylor & Francis Group

LONDON AND NEW YORK

First published 2020
by Routledge
2 Park Square, Milton Park, Abingdon, Oxon OX14 4RN

and by Routledge
52 Vanderbilt Avenue, New York, NY 10017

Routledge is an imprint of the Taylor & Francis Group, an informa business

British Library Cataloguing in Publication Data
A catalogue record for this book is available from the British Library

Library of Congress Cataloging in Publication Data
Names: Klassen, Thomas Richard, 1957– author. |
Menges, Christine, 1978– author.
Title: The essential guide to studying abroad : from
success in the classroom to a fulfilling career /
by Thomas R. Klassen and Christine Menges.
Description: Abingdon, Oxon ; New York, NY : Routledge, 2020. |
Includes bibliographical references.
Identifiers: LCCN 2019015317 | ISBN 9780367235154 (hardback) |
ISBN 9780367235161 (pbk.) | ISBN 9780429280115 (ebook)
Subjects: LCSH: Foreign study–Handbooks, manuals, etc.
Classification: LCC LB2375 .K52 2020 | DDC 370.116–dc23
LC record available at https://lccn.loc.gov/2019015317

ISBN: 978-0-367-23515-4 (hbk)
ISBN: 978-0-367-23516-1 (pbk)
ISBN: 978-0-429-28011-5 (ebk)

Typeset in Palatino
by Newgen Publishing UK

To my wife Sue Han, and our children Claire Alexandra Yon-Ah Han and Alexander Richard Jun-Won Klassen

Thomas R. Klassen

and

To my husband Jochen, and our children Elisa, Emily, and Henry, and my parents Wolfgang and Elsie

Christine Menges

Contents

Illustrations

Figures

Tables

Preface

We wrote this book to ensure that international students flourish during their time abroad, and succeed after graduation. The chapters that follow assist international students to succeed in their applications to study abroad; flourish in the classroom of their new home; and obtain a fulfilling job after graduation. Our advice comes from our own experience and that of the hundreds of international students we have taught, counselled, and otherwise assisted in North America, Europe, and Asia. Our counsel also derives from officials in university admission offices and selection committees, student advisers, and employers on all continents who hire graduates who are international students. Our scholarly research on international students, and more generally on student success, finds expression in the chapter that follow. Lastly, we've let international student tell their own stories, which are found as case studies throughout the book.

We are grateful to colleagues and students at the University of Toronto and York University (in Canada), Anglia Ruskin University and City University, London (England), University of St. Gallen (Switzerland), Yonsei University (South Korea), University of Konstanz and WHU – Otto Beisheim School of Management (Germany), and University of the Philippines. Our time in these institutions of higher learning has allowed us to experience first-hand being an international student, and also teaching and supporting international students.

We are also indebted to the Academy of Korean Studies for funding (grant AKS-2017-R-50) that allowed us to conduct in-depth research on the experience of international students.

Some parts of this book are drawn from *How to Succeed at University (and Get a Great Job!): Mastering the Critical Skills You Need for School, Work and Life* (2015) authored by Thomas R. Klassen and John A. Dwyer. This material is used with permission of the Publisher, University of British Columbia Press. All rights reserved by the Publisher. That book is also available in French as *Décrocher son diplôme universitaire (et l'emploi de vos rêves!): Comment maîtriser les compétences essentielles menant au succès à l'école, au travail et dans la vie* (2018) translated by Émilie Laramée. We express our thanks to the authors and publishers for being able to adapt material from these publications.

We are especially grateful to the following colleagues and former students from around the world who have read parts of the book, contributed comments and case studies, and otherwise contributed to its content: Nadia Alacorn, Paul Carr, Haneul Choi, Romy Darius, Daniel Enzinger, Maria Mercedes Bacadare Goitia, Phillip Haas, Meiyu Huang, Anthony Karge, Miriam Kraneis, Christina Ljubic, Valentina Nahuero, Nkechi Nwokoye, Goran Popovic, Shruti Ravuri, Anna Riepe, Thaysa Salgado, Sayalee Shende, Vivek Singh, James Soto, Suramya Tyagi, and Grace Yau. The three anonymous reviewers of the manuscript provided extraordinarily helpful and insightful recommendations and counsel. Their comments and suggestions on how to improve our presentation and explanation have made this a much stronger final product.

Lastly, we are indebted to Yongling Lam, Samantha Phua, and their colleagues at Routledge for their roles in bringing this book to you, as well as Kelly Winter and her colleagues at Newgen Publishing UK for the copyediting, typesetting and proofreading.

Thomas R. Klassen, PhD
Toronto, Canada and Seoul, South Korea

Christine Menges, PhD
Düsseldorf, Germany

Introduction

Optimizing success as an international student

Twenty years from now you will be more disappointed by the things you didn't do, than by the ones you did do.

Mark Twain

Introduction

You're reading this page because you wish to be an international student, or perhaps already are. Possibly you've found this book because you teach international students, or in other ways work to ensure their success as a counsellor or adviser. Or, you're here because you are the parent of a young person contemplating studying abroad.

International students are growing in number, and studying abroad has become an option for more and more students. Many governments and post-secondary institutions have extensive programmes – such as scholarships – to both attract students from abroad and to encourage local students to study in another country. Some countries and universities offer free tuition to international students.

Yet, many students are unsure if they should study abroad, and when they do study away from their home country they are not fully prepared to flourish in their new environment and to succeed after graduation. At times those who want to help prospective international students – parents and grandparents, school counsellors, and advisers – are not quite sure how to proceed.

The objectives of the book are to: (1) ensure that you succeed in your studies as an international student or as a prospective international learner, while also having the most fantastic time of your life; and (2) make certain that you can leverage your international study experience to obtain a promising career after graduation in a global workforce.

This book is unique in showing you where to invest your energy to get the best results during all stages of international studies: from application to starting a rewarding career after graduation. In the chapters that follow you will learn what to do, how do to it, and reasons why it works.

Why international studies?

In 2018 there were more than five million international students with half of these studying in English speaking countries. Two decades earlier there were less than two million international students. In business terminology, studying abroad is a growth industry.[1] There are good reasons for that.[2]

Studying abroad has become an option for more students than ever before. The world is more global than ever before.[3] Business and economics, science, entertainment, and much more operate at an international scale.

Having the good fortune to experience first-hand the language, traditions, and different ways of life by being immersed in a new country as a student changed my life. It lead me to settle in my new home for one year after completing my undergraduate degree. Both as a student, and then as a worker, I encountered people, places, and events that taught me lessons I otherwise would have never received and learned.

Living in a country where I didn't speak the language was beyond difficult, but it sharpened my problem-solving skills and gave me the confidence to take risks that got me to amazing places. Staying in my comfort zone would have meant missing out on so very much of what I treasure, and what now makes me special.

Nkechi Nwokoye

Higher education plays a crucial role in ensuring that young people are ready for the complexities of work and responsive to societal needs. University graduates enter a global workforce that is changing rapidly and is highly competitive, as a result of advances in technology and increased mobility. Students and parents know that employers place a premium on new professionals who have a wide range of skills including adaptability, problem-solving, critical thinking, and intercultural awareness.

One way to develop these sought-after skills is through studying abroad. International study comes in an astounding variety of packages: from a few weeks during the summer to many years. You can complete one course abroad, a semester or a year, or an entire degree. Some students begin international studies right after completing high school, while others do so after completing a university degree. As for the location, the world is your destination with nearly every country offering international students a place.

Many countries openly welcome and court international students. The US, Canada, the UK, and Australia, among others, have long-standing policies to attract international students.[4] Many of the universities and colleges in those countries offer appealing scholarships and other financial support.

However, don't simply focus on studying in highly developed Western nations. Recently more countries in Asia, such as China, as well as South America and the Caribbean have also sought to attract international students. Some institutions in those nations also offer generous financial aid. In many cases, these countries have low living costs, which is something to consider. Have you considered African nations for your study abroad experience?

Figure 1.1 in the Appendix at the end of this chapter shows you the countries that have the most international students (in proportion to all the students in that country). Figure 1.1 also shows you that studying abroad for a Master's degree or PhD is very common.

Certain languages are essential to succeed in careers with multinational corporations or international agencies, especially English. The best way to master a language is to be fully immersed in it. Not surprisingly, more than half of all international students study in English-speaking nations.

English is the majority or official language in many nations apart from the US, Canada, the UK, Australia, and New Zealand. Countries such as Singapore, The Bahamas, Belize, Philippines, Ghana, and others have universities that operate largely in English, and populations where many people speak English. In addition, many universities in Europe offer programmes in English.[5]

Studying outside of your own country – whether for a few weeks, a summer, a semester, a year, or longer – is a wonderful way to learn about the world. For many young people it is the most amazing adventure ever! Learning in a classroom is necessary and useful, but studying abroad also means learning about a new culture and making friends.

You can learn history or biology from a book or video, but add that to walking through the ruins or in the rainforest and the experience becomes richer and more intense. Learning outside the box and expanding your horizons is more likely to happen when you're in a new environment. Finally, learning abroad includes learning about yourself, such as confronting new situations, challenging yourself, or pursuing avenues that were closed to you at home.

Studying abroad was an unforgettable time of my life. Being part of a different culture and getting a grade while having fun was the best decision I made in my young adult life.

I decided to study abroad because of academic problems, including grades that were not up to par with my peers. One of my instructors told me to drop out of university and reconsider my plans to earn a degree. I felt like I had hit rock bottom.

It was at that time that I discovered my school had summer study abroad courses in which I could travel and get a grade. I grabbed that chance in a heartbeat.

> I smiled more during the study abroad course than in any other. Being in a country half-way around the world and learning something new every minute – inside and outside the classroom – was such a thrill.
> Studying abroad gave me a whole new perspective transforming not only my school life, but also my way of thinking about the world and my place in it.
>
> James Soto

In this book we use the term "international student" rather than "foreign student" (although sometimes "foreign student" does creep in). "Foreign" has multiple meanings such as different, alien or strange; which have nothing at all to do with being a young person studying in another country. "International," meaning global and between nations, is more commonly used these days, and without the negative connotations of "foreign."

This book also uses the term "university" to encompass a whole range of places of higher learning: colleges, schools, institutes, academies, and others. At times, we use the term "institution" to refer to these places.

We've written this book in a way that you can apply it to your own life regardless of whether you are beginning to contemplate studying abroad, or about to graduate. You may be the first person in your family, or among your friends, or among your classmates, to study abroad. That does not mean you need to do it all alone. Use this book as a companion in your journey. Even if you have others to advise and guide you, this book will offer you valuable insights and resources.

Where to find what

This book is written in an accessible style that assumes you might read the contents in one go, or alternatively read individual chapters or sections as they apply to your life. Each chapter has tips and real-world examples, as well as links to online resources and notes at the end of each chapter that point to additional interesting reading which you can pursue if time permits. Moreover, international students tell their own stories in the case studies that are sprinkled throughout the book.

Chapter 2 prepares you for international studies, including how to maximize the success of your application. Studying abroad takes considerable planning. This chapter shows you how to write an amazing statement of interest, get the best possible letters of reference and increase your chances of being accepted into the programme of your choice.

Money is crucial for an international education. The chapter helps you to understand scholarships, bursaries and grants, and how to apply for these. Following the advice in the chapter will maximize your chances of obtaining money to pay for your studies.

Chapter 3 starts from when you step off the plane (or train or ship or car) into your new environment. Things will be new and exciting, and sometimes a little scary as well. This chapter will make sure that your new life begins smoothly and you're soon having the time of your life, and that the inevitable problems that you encounter will not derail you. Included in this chapter are topics such as how to interact with professors in your new university and how to make friends.

Chapter 4 teaches you how to excel at exams and writing assignments at your new school in order to earn the best grades possible. Tests, exams, and writing assignments are difficult at the best of times, but even more so in a new environment and in a language that might be new to you. The chapter shares some secrets and hints to make exams and writing assignments much easier, and how to avoid common problems faced by international students, such as plagiarism.

Chapter 5 is focused on tasks that all students usually try to avoid, especially international learners, namely presentations in front of others, and teamwork. But, after reading the chapter you may even have fun with these activities! You will also understand how and why they are crucial in other parts of your life. The chapter will aid you in becoming an even more proactive and high-performing student in the classroom and outside.

Chapter 6 begins the second part of the book: the transition from school to work. The chapter starts from when you realize that your university studies are soon coming to an end and you need to prepare for full-time post-education work. All the time and energy invested in learning abroad will mean little if you don't have meaningful opportunities to apply the knowledge.

After reading Chapter 6 you will have identified your values, interests, personality, and skills that will guide you in finding a great job after graduation. By following the self-assessments in the chapter you will better understand your unique characteristics and the most suitable employment opportunities available to you. Lastly, the chapter teaches you how to discover where the jobs are using informational interviews, as well as social media platforms such as LinkedIn.

Chapter 7 will allow you to craft a résumé that gets you noticed by potential employers. We make writing a résumé a less frustrating task for you by providing you with advice based on our experience working with many different types of international students. Plenty of real-world examples, as well as online resources, are found in this chapter.

Chapter 8 takes you through interviews so that by the end of the chapter you will never fear them again. The focus of the chapter is how to ensure that potential employers recognize and reward you for your hard work as an international student. After reading the chapter, you will know exactly what questions to expect in an interview, and how to answer them.

Chapter 9 takes you to the world of full-time permanent employment whether in your home country, host country, or elsewhere, and explains how to ensure your success in the years to come. You'll see that your time abroad has given you an advantage that will last for many years and that you can build on as you progress in your career.

In 2016, I decided to take a study abroad course based in South Korea. It was my first time overseas and I wasn't sure what to expect. Being a foreigner in a new environment was a humbling experience for me. Things were different, yet the same.

During my time in South Korea, I formed new friendships, ventured out of my comfort zone by experiencing Korean culture first-hand, and learned the Korean language. Although I am different racially and culturally from a native Korean, I discovered that it was the human experience that helped me form an appreciation and deep respect for the country.

Studying abroad left such an impact on my life that I returned to South Korea in 2017 to work as an English teacher and I am now pursuing my MA in International Relations at one of Korea's top universities via the Korean Government Scholarship Program.

I can't imagine what my life would be like had I not made the decision to study abroad. The opportunities that have sprung forth from it have immeasurably blessed my life.

Romy Darius

A note for parents and others

For parents, international study can often be more unnerving than for students. Hearing from a son or daughter of his or her plans to study in another land can come as a surprise or even shock. The same might apply if your spouse or significant other has plans to study abroad. You may not even be familiar with the university, city, or country that your child or significant other is planning to attend.

Any parent or spouse in such a situation will have questions (e.g. "What will it cost?") and concerns (e.g. "But, you're so young!" and "Are you coming back home after you finish your studies?"). These are entirely understandable and indeed should be the questions you ask.

This book is designed to help you better understand the international study experience. In this way, you can be sure to ask the right questions. More importantly, this book offers your child the skills, competence, and information to answer your questions and respond to your concerns.

Sometimes, parents say "Why are you doing this?" In our experience, most parents can answer that question on their own. Did you not once consider international study or point to its benefits? Don't you wish you had done something similar some decades ago or even more recently? The quotation that starts this chapter draws attention to looking at post-secondary education from a long-term perspective.

Parents often feel that their child is too young to benefit from studying abroad, but consider that the experience is designed for young adults who are eager to learn. University campuses are safe environments and there are steps that students can – and should – take to ensure their health and safety while abroad (see Chapter 3).

Studying abroad is easier than ever. This in itself reduces stress for parents, grandparents, and others. You can easily stay in contact via social media. Speaking to your child in another continent is no more difficult or expensive than if she or he was a few blocks from home.

Relatively low-cost airfare means that a flight to visit your child, or for your child to visit you (especially at off-peak times) is more affordable than ever before. This can give reassurance to parents.

Studying abroad is also more common than ever.[6] Until three to four decades ago international study was largely reserved for the well-to-do. Travel was expensive, making financial transactions across borders was complicated, and relatively few universities sought international students.

If you are unsure of how to proceed, talk to other parents or friends. What experiences have they had? What would they do in a similar situation?

Plans for international study may raise topics in your family that you've not previously discussed. Perhaps there is only one international study opportunity that your family can reasonably afford, but you have several school-age children. Who gets to go?

Or you may conclude that your child lacks the maturity at the moment to benefit from learning abroad or you may feel that your child could find herself or himself in situations she or he is not prepared to deal with. Or you may decide that the location the child prefers for international study is unsuitable.

Alternatively, you may believe that your child should start international study, but encounter resistance from him or her or from school counsellors and officials. Lastly, your child may have a learning disability or have another disability that could impact his or her success in studying abroad. You would like him or her to be independent and strong, but worry that he or she may not be able to manage in the new environment.

These are difficult situations to deal with. Patience and a willingness to compromise will help you make the best decisions for your child and your family.

Regardless of your unique circumstances as a parent, grandparent, or guardian, this book will be of value. Our hope is that using this book you and your child can collaborate to make her or his international study experience splendid in every way possible.

Appendix 1

Figure 1.1 shows – in the tinted bars – the percentage of university students in a country who are international students. For example, in Luxembourg, nearly 50 per cent of all university students are international students. In Australia, nearly 30 per cent of all students are international students, while the figure for France is 10 per cent.

The figure also shows – using diamonds, circles and triangles – how many international students are enrolled in bachelor programmes, Master programmes and Doctoral (PhD) programmes in each country. For example, in the US, 40 per cent of all PhD students are international students while only 10 per cent of all Master's students are international students.

Use the information to give you a sense of how many students (as a percentage of all students) are international students in a country, and also how many students studying for a particular type of degree are international students.

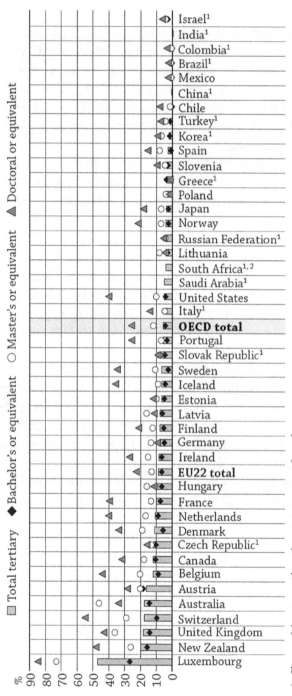

■ Total tertiary   ◆ Bachelor's or equivalent   ○ Master's or equivalent   ▲ Doctoral or equivalent

1. Share of foreign rather than international students.
2. Year of reference 2015.

Countries are ranked in descending order of the percentage of international or foreign students in tertiary education.

Figure 1.1 International university students as a percentage of all university students in a country, 2016
Source: Figure B6.1 page 218 of OECD, *Education at a Glance 2018: OECD Indicators* (Paris: OECD, 2018).

Notes

1   For more information and data about international students, and post-secondary education around the world, please see the publication by the Organisation for Economic Co-operation and Development (OECD) titled *Education at a Glance 2018: OECD Indicators*. This is available at: https://read.oecd-ilibrary.org/education/education-at-a-glance-2018_eag-2018-en#page1

2   To understand some of the global trends that impact international students, look at Rahul Choudaha, "Three Waves of International Student Mobility (1999–2020)," *Studies in Higher Education*, 42(5) (2017): 825–832. doi: 10.1080/03075079.2017.1293872.

3   Globalization is one of the key features of our times. Read more about what this really means at: Mauro F. Guillén, "Is Globalization Civilizing, Destructive or Feeble? A Critique of Five Key Debates in the Social Science Literature," *Annual Review of Sociology*, 27 (2003): 235–260. doi: 10.1146/annurev.soc.27.1.235.

4   To see how politics and economics play a role in which countries recruit international students, see Creso M. Sá and Emma Sabzalieva, "The Politics of the Great Brain Race: Public Policy and International Student Recruitment in Australia, Canada, England and the USA," *Higher Education*, 75(2) (2018): 231–253.

5   To learn about how English became so widespread see David Crystal, *English as a Global Language* (Cambridge: Cambridge University Press, 2012).

6   Jennifer A. Pope, et al., "Why Do Gen Y Students Study Abroad? Individual Growth and the Intent to Study Abroad," *Journal of Teaching in International Business*, 25(2) (2014): 97–118. doi: 10.1080/08975930.2014.896232.

Succeeding in your studies
Applying, adjusting, and mastering

CHAPTER 2

Preparing for international learning

It always seems impossible until it's done.
Nelson Mandela

Introduction

Sometimes young people interested in studying abroad have difficulty knowing how to get started, and that is entirely understandable. Planning to study abroad can seem daunting at the start. After all, there is a whole world and moving away from home can be scary.

If you've never been an international student before: everything is new! So, let's take things one step at a time.

Your passion for international studies

The first step is to better understand where your desire to study elsewhere comes from. Have you had a long-standing desire to learn a particular language or culture? Or is it because of what friends have reported to you about their experiences living in another country? Or your parents think studying abroad is a good idea? Or you would like a fresh start where no one knows you?

You can classify reasons into *pull* factors and *push* factors. Pull factors are those tugging you to study abroad: perhaps an exotic locale, the opportunity of a scholarship, or the chance to learn a language and make new friends.

Push factors are those shoving you away from your current situation. Maybe you're miserable with your current courses and degree, or unhappy about living at home, or worried about your post-graduation employment options.

All reasons are valid and important ones, but it helps to understand what they are before you begin the journey.

When I decided to spend a semester studying in Thailand, I wasn't thinking about my long-term career goals. As a 20-year-old on the verge of graduating, a semester abroad seemed like a respectable excuse to visit Asia for the first time.

Many of the other exchange students in the programme had the same idea: a fun semester abroad, some travel, and then head back home. Sure, maybe we'd come back for a vacation in the future, but that would be it.

That's what I thought at the time, at least. Being exposed to the region, with its welcoming culture and dynamic economy, made an impact on me. So much of an impact that I felt the inescapable urge to return to the region.

After a handful of years of working back in my home country, I returned to the region. My experience in Thailand helped me land a job in neighbouring Cambodia. I spent two years working full-time to help a nonprofit scale its fundraising efforts. It was great to be back in the region, and even better to be there in a longer-term capacity while developing my skills.

My time in Cambodia motivated me to seek a master's degree to further my interest in marketing. All of this happened because of one semester abroad. What I thought was just going to be a fun diversion ended up being a defining experience.

Anthony Karge

What and where?

The next step is to consider the options you have for international studies. Perhaps there is only enough time for a summer semester.

Or, you would like to study abroad for a year or an entire degree? Don't limit yourself at the start of your thinking and planning.

If you are currently a student at a university or college, look for your international studies office. The staff and online resources will help you by showing the options your university has already prepared. Most universities have agreements with partner institutions abroad. The agreements will make your study abroad experience smoother and easier. Look at the list of universities that have partner agreements.

If you are currently in high school, check out your guidance office and speak to your teachers. Searching online is also a great way to obtain general knowledge about your study abroad options.

You can also talk with your professors and teachers. They can make useful recommendations. But, avoid going to see them with vague questions like "I'm thinking about studying somewhere else, but am not sure. What should I do?" Rather, go to your history teacher with a specific question like "I'm keen on learning more about classical Greek culture by studying abroad. Might you be able to recommend universities and programmes in Greece?"

The most valuable advice you will get is from other international students. Find them online, or from your group of friends or work colleagues, or family members. Get feedback from people who are similar to you in age, background, and interests.

An online search for the best universities for "foreign students" or "international students" will help you as well, and expand your perspective. But remember, that the definition of "best university" will vary greatly.

Interestingly, the ranking of the top 200 universities with the most foreign students conducted by the *Times Higher Education* magazine places the American University of Sharjah in the United Arab Emirates first.[1] Who knew?

You may have cities, regions, or countries that you've always dreamed you would visit and live in, or particular universities that have held a long attraction. Alternatively, you may be quite open and flexible about the location, but have a particular programme or area of studies that is at the top of your list.

Slowly develop a list of possible universities based on your interests, time frame, and agreements that your current university may have in place if you are currently enrolled in school. Keep an open mind at this time as the list may change as you move through the next steps.

Money

International study takes some money. But don't be discouraged with your venture due to money as you will likely be surprised at the ways you can receive financial help for your studies. In many cases some costs will be covered by your current university (if you are an exchange student). Many universities are keen to entice international students who are applying straight from high school with tuition waivers, scholarships, or other sources of funding. Financial assistance is even more abundant for those applying for Master's and PhD programmes.

You will need to do research on the particular programme or institution you are interested in. Be warned that you will not find this on a single website, and also be aware that fees and financial assistance programmes change each year.

As you learn more about the costs, you might revise your list of universities or programmes that appeal to you. But as you learn about costs also start to conduct research on how to minimize these. You will be astounded with what you will find. Searching for "scholarships for international students" on Google.com returns more than 125 million hits.

Websites such as www.internationalstudent.com/scholarships allow you to search international student scholarships by location, subject of study, and student origin. Don't use websites that ask you for payment. You can easily find everything you need on your own.

Various organizations and groups offer funds specifically for international students. Look at funding offered by Rotary International as an example.[2]

You may be eligible for funding because of where you are planning to study, or the specific programme, or due to other characteristics. Again, research will help you locate funds.

Some students are interested in studying in nations or locales with which they have a personal connection. For example, you might wish to study in the land that one of your parents was born. If that is the case, check if you might be eligible for citizenship in that country or some other consideration, which will reduce your tuition fees and other costs.

Be flexible in searching for funds and remember that information found online is a guideline, not something carved in stone.

Understanding funding

There are four sources of funding available to you (other than your own and that of your family) for studying abroad:

1.   Funding from the university you plan to attend.
2.   Funding from external sources.
3.   Funding from your current university to study abroad (if you are presently a student).
4.   Money earned as a research or teaching assistant if you are a Master's or PhD student.

Regardless of the source of funding, it will come in one of the following types.

- **Scholarships** or prizes are offered due to academic, athletic, or other types of excellence.
- **Bursaries** are offered on the basis of financial need. Usually you must demonstrate that you need the funds to receive bursaries.
- **Grants**, sometimes also called awards, are offered for specific reasons, such as to encourage international students to attend an institution, or to encourage students to pursue a particular programme of studies.

In many cases, if you are awarded a scholarship, you will not see the money. In other words, the money will flow directly to the university you are attending to cover some, or all of, your tuition or accommodation costs.

Scholarships, bursaries, and grants are offered by many organizations including, of course, universities, but also private sector organizations like companies and employers, industry associations, professional associations, labour unions, sport and athletics associations, governments, religious groups, charitable organizations, and many, many more.

Employment as a research or teaching assistant is usually reserved for graduate students; that is those you have already earned an undergraduate or first degree. In some cases you might be guaranteed such employment when you are admitted to a programme, while in other cases you need to apply once you begin your studies.

How to apply

Applications for these wonderful sources of funds are usually in one of two forms. First, you may be considered automatically for scholarships, bursaries, and grants (as well as employment if you are a graduate student) by the university you are applying to. In other words, the university will use the documents that you submit when you apply to also determine if you are eligible for funding.

For you, this is the ideal situation as no further work is required on your part. But, in many cases the university will have additional sources of funding that you need to apply to specifically. Check for these!

> **TIP 2.1** Every year in almost every university around the world some scholarships, bursaries, and grants are not distributed for the sole reason that no one applied!

And, all scholarships, bursaries, and grants offered by organizations other than your intended university will require individual applications. Yes, lots of work but certainly worthwhile.

Each application will be a little different, but you will soon see the patterns. This will make the effort much less on your part.

When you look for sources of funds, don't be shy! Ask around. Certainly be sure to ask your current university (if you have one), and the university and programme you are applying to. You may well be pleasantly surprised, and the very worst that can happen is being told "Sorry, no!"

Be strategic. Once you have a list of all of the sources of financial aid to which you can apply, look for the ones that seem most relevant to you. In other words, those that you are most likely to secure!

Scholarships can be related to your academic performance, but there are also plenty of scholarships that take into account other activities: sports and athletics, community contributions, language skills, and much more. Bursaries and grants have wide ranging eligibility criteria including the location of your birth to your education and career interests.

The grades or other requirements that you may find in scholarship, bursary, and grant application documents are usually flexible. You have everything to gain from applying, even if you think you don't meet all the eligibility requirements.

Fortunately, the application process for scholarships, bursaries, and grants is pretty well the same you have followed, or will need to follow, to apply to universities. The same documents are needed. See later in this chapter for what is needed and how to prepare the most compelling funding applications.

The deadlines for scholarships will likely be different from the deadline to apply to universities. You may find yourself applying for scholarships or bursaries before you applied to the university, and even know if you have even been accepted.

Obstacles

You may be pleasantly surprised – or unpleasantly – once you start to compile a budget of what an international education will cost. The exchange rate between your home currency and that of your location may not be in your favour. Items like books, food, and others may be more expensive in the location you are planning to study than in your home country.

If you start to feel depressed that your international study plans are blocked because of money, then take a step back. Can you be more flexible about your goals? If needed, can you wait a year and use it to save money? Are there things you are willing to give up for an international education? Are there other countries or programmes you can consider where the cost is lower?

Our experience is that very few young people are entirely prevented from studying abroad. Your plans may need to be adjusted, but rarely abandoned. You might consider working holiday programmes that are offered in some countries, as an entry to studying abroad.

Hiring an agent

Some students, or their families, hire an agent to manage the application process and related matters associated with an international education such as scholarships. This makes sense in cases where the cost of the international education is high (like an entire degree) or where there are language barriers. Obtaining paid assistance is also helpful in cases where there are special needs or conditions related to visas or other matters. The agents are usually experienced and can minimize the time involved.

However, most students (and their families) do not need professional aid, and universities don't expect you to have this to pursue an international education. Nearly all English-speaking universities make sure that their application procedures are sufficiently accessible for most young people to undertake on their own.

TIP 2.2 As you complete your application, you may start to feel that your chances of being accepted will increase if you wrote to some of the professors at the university you are applying to. Unless you are a PhD student or applying for a very specialized programme, there is no need to do this.

Professors are busy people and hearing from applicants who may arrive on campus some many months in the future is not high on their list of priorities. Rather, professors are focused on the students they are currently teaching.

There is little, if anything, that a professor can do for an applicant. So, if you do write, expect (at most) a short message saying that the professor would be happy to hear from you once you have been admitted to the university and are on campus.

One day during my studies, I felt the need for some fresh air and applied for a semester in Madrid. Spontaneously! It was the very last day to hand in applications for the upcoming exchange and because I was the only applicant from my batch, I was accepted even though I failed the language test.

Honestly, my Spanish skills were hardly enough to successfully order a beer, but I wanted to escape Germany for a while, so I just booked a flight and arrived in Madrid some weeks later.

I had to organize a place to live in Madrid communicating through visual gestures and single words I found in a dictionary. I remember quite interesting "talks" to landlords until I found a little room.

In Spain, I went through lots of such situations – always knowing I would manage them somehow. I never lost that optimism.

Once I graduated and started full-time work, my employer sent me to Hungary to train blue-collar workers on complex and sophisticated welding machines. Remembering my time in Spain, I kept calm and succeeded in my job even without being able to speak Hungarian.

Phillip Haas

Using a "do-it-yourself" approach you will need to do research on your own and you may need help from others such as friends, family members, classmates, and others who have studied abroad. The internet will be a surprisingly valuable tool. Of course, if things become overwhelming or you encounter impassable barriers, then asking for professional assistance is quite fine. If you do, look for reputable agents, ideally those who have helped other international applicants whom you know. Be sure to understand what you are paying for and how things will unfold.

Applications

Once you've decided on your preferred study abroad location(s), the next step is to apply. In some cases, such as if you are already a university student, you may only need one application that your home university will use for you as an exchange student.

If you are beginning university studies, or are applying for a Master's or PhD programme, you will likely apply for several universities, as you are not sure of being accepted. Deciding how many applications to submit is difficult to know. Each application takes time and money.

The general rule is to apply to between three and five institutions. If you apply to fewer than three you may not be accepted. If you apply to more than five you've not done enough research to know which universities and programmes are a good fit for you.

Fortunately, the application process for all institutions is pretty similar. You will need to submit:

1. A statement of interest or intent.
2. Letters of reference or recommendation from people who know you.
3. A sample of work you've done, such as an essay or other assignment.
4. Your transcript(s).
5. Results from standardized academic and language tests.
6. Your résumé (see Chapter 7).

These are the same documents that you need when applying for scholarships or other sources of funding.

All six components are important, but what will get you accepted or rejected – or get you a scholarship or not – are the first two: the statement of interest, and the letters of reference. They are the crucial parts of the application.

Let's look at each of the six components in turn.

Statement of interest

Nearly all applications for study abroad opportunities ask you to write a letter of statement of interest. That is, to explain why you wish to become an international student.

If you can submit a compelling statement of interest, you have a very good probability of being accepted. Moreover, you may also be offered some financial assistance. A weak statement of interest has the opposite effect.

Statements of interest are hard to write because you have only a few hundred words to explain yourself, perhaps using a language in which you are not fluent. Composing your statement of interest is one of the hardest writing assignments. Here's how to do it well.

Most people write statements of interest chronologically. They start with "I was born ..." and proceed to the present. But that's not the way to write a compelling statement.

The readers of the statement have little interest in your past and your present, rather they want to hear about your future. Specifically, they want to learn three things: (1) what motivates you to pursue an international education; (2) how prepared you are to succeed in your studies; and (3) your plans for the future.

Start the statement at the present time, or even in the future. For example:

> In five years I will be working for an international aid organiza-
> tion in Africa helping to reduce poverty among young mothers.
> To prepare me to succeed in my career, I plan to spend a year
> studying abroad to learn about life in a developing country to
> supplement my classroom education.

Compare that to:

> I was born the youngest child of parents who worked hard to
> provide an education for their children. In high school I took
> extra classes in English and volunteered on the student news-
> paper. After high school I was fortunate to be accepted into a
> good university. I did not do well in my first year of studies due
> to stress and not knowing what courses to take.

Which statement is more powerful, compelling, and interesting? Which statement demonstrates more maturity? Which statement is from a person who is most likely to succeed in studying abroad?

Remember that the people reading your statement will have dozens, perhaps hundreds, and possibly thousands of statements to read.

TIP 2.3 Do not spend time explaining poor academic perform-ance in your statement of interest. Don't include sentences such as "I did not earn good grades because ..." Stay positive, and demonstrate what you can do, and more importantly what you wish to do.

There is no particular format or structure for a statement of interest. It needs to reflect who you are. But it does have to be written as clearly as possible. As we noted above, the readers will have many statements to read, and if yours is confusing or unclear, it will just be put aside.

Here's how to craft the statement that reflects your strengths.

1. Before writing, think about what is your main message. You want to be accepted into the programme or university, but that is not the main message. Why do you want to be accepted? Surely because you want to make a difference in the years to come in your field of study.
2. Clearly express how being an international student will play a role in your future. Will the experience allow you to do things you could not otherwise?
3. Demonstrate an authentic fascination for whatever subject or programme you are applying for, and for the country and city of the institution you wish to attend.
4. Avoid careless words, such as "There are countless reasons why I want to study at your university." Is there number of reasons really countless?
5. Don't pander and suck up. Avoid phrases like "attending your programme is the only dream I have in my life." Keep the statement professional in all aspects. Remember that the readers will be a group of professors!

Lastly, remember, focus on the future. The past is the past. The people reading the statement are interested in the kind of person you are right now and even more so the kind of person you will be in several months and years from now.

Letters of reference or recommendation

Letters of reference from past or current teachers, employers, and others who know you can make or break international study applications. These letters will also be essential for obtaining a great job after you complete your university education.

Here's how to get the best possible letters.

It can be confusing figuring out who to ask for letters of reference. Is it a current teacher or a former teacher, a current employer or a past one, or a religious or community leader, or a friend or family member?

Look at the international study application requirements. These will give you instructions about the number of letters of reference required and who should write them. But, don't worry if you cannot exactly fit the requirements.

Don't obtain letters from friends or family members, no matter how prestigious the person's position might be. Letters of reference from friends, friends of your family, or family members usually have little credibility.

Of course, there might be times when there is no way around this. If you're asked to include a letter from an employer, and your only employer has been a family member, then it is acceptable to have this individual write a letter of recommendation for you.

For the most part you will be asking current or former teachers and professors for a letter of reference. The good thing is that writing letters of reference is part of the job of being a teacher and you'll find that few will decline to do this for you.

However, teachers have many students each year or term, and may not remember enough about you to write you a strong letter. It may have been several years since you were taught by a specific teacher. Help the person – whether teacher, employer, or community leader – write you a convincing letter by:

1. providing details about where you are applying and why, including the website address for your study abroad programme/university;
2. including your statement of interest even if only a draft;
3. sending your transcript showing your courses and grades, highlighting the courses you took with your recommender,

the grades you earned in the courses, and the topics and grades of assignments you wrote;

4. enclosing a copy of your résumé; and
5. attaching a sample of your work (the same sample that you will include in your application package, if required).

Asking for a letter of reference can be uncomfortable or even nerve-wracking. Here's how to do it. First, send a short email – this is less stressful than walking up to someone. Use this sample and adapt it to your particular circumstances:

Dear Professor Walters:

I was a student in your class "International Law" in the 2018 January to May semester.

I am applying for international studies at three universities in Australia for my MA in anthropology. As part of the application process I have been asked to arrange letters of reference. Would you be willing to write these for me? The letters are due by October 31st and must be submitted via an online portal. You will be sent an email from the universities that I am applying to with details on how to complete the letters.

If you are willing to write the letters, I will provide you with more information about the programme I am applying to, including my (1) draft statement of interest, (2) transcript, (3) résumé, and (4) information about the course I took with you, including the assignments I completed.

I would be pleased to meet with you at your convenience to provide you with additional information, or answer any questions you may have.

Thank you,

[your name and student number]

As indicated in the sample above, always offer to meet the person. In some cases this is essential, in other cases less so.

Second, if the person agrees to write the recommendation letter, submit the materials with a second email. In this email quickly summarize what you think are your strong points. For example:

Dear Professor Walters:

Thank you very much for agreeing to write a letter of reference for my application for MA studies in Australia.

Please find attached my draft statement of interest, my transcript, my résumé, as well as information about the course I took with you including the assignments I completed. More information about the programmes that I am applying to in Australia is at: www.australia.program

I took your course "International Law" in the 2018 January to May semester. My final paper for the course was titled "The Failure of International Law for Refugees in Asia-Pacific." You gave my paper a grade of 83 per cent and wrote in your comments: "This is an excellent third-year paper that demonstrates considerable research and careful writing. Perhaps one day you will explore this topic further."

You recall that two other students in the class (May Chung and Will Brontis) and I prepared an oral presentation on "Refugee Law and Aboriginal Peoples" on March 18th. In your comments on the presentation you wrote: "You have worked very well as a team to share your knowledge. Your presentation kept the attention of the audience throughout."

You will receive an email directly from the three Australian universities with instructions on how to prepare and submit the reference letter.

Again, thank you very much for your assistance. I will make sure to let you know the result of my application.

Sincerely,

[your name and student number]

Submit your requests for letters of recommendation at least four weeks in advance of their due date. Then two weeks before send a reminder to the person. The people writing the letters for you are busy and writing your letter may not be their first priority.

Lastly, once you are notified that the letter of recommendation has been sent and received, send a nice note of thanks to your letter writer. This can be an email, or perhaps a paper note or card.

It is hard to decide who to ask for letters. You may have taken a course with a professor you really liked and you are sure they remember you, but your performance in the class was just average. On the other hand, you took a large course that you did very well in, but the professor is unlikely to remember you.

That is a tough situation. Our general advice is to go with the professor who knows you better. By providing them with the additional documents outlined above they will see the kind of person you are now: organized, and highly motivated.

From our experience detailed and nuanced letters of recommendation from people who know you well are read more carefully and seen more positively compared to standard and generic letters – even if more glowing – from someone who does not know you very well.

Below are two letters of recommendation drawn from real world letters we have seen. Which one was more effective in making sure the applicant is accepted?

Letter A:
"Andrei C. was a fine student who submitted all the required work for the course. I highly recommend him."

Letter B:
"Andrew R. came to meet with me early in the term. The course he took from me required knowledge that he had not learned in previous courses. He understood that he would have to invest extra time and effort in the course and that the first two assignments would be particularly difficult for him and would not earn strong grades.

I was delighted to see that he improved steadily as the course progressed and mastered the material by the completion of the course. I should add that during the final weeks of the course he spent time assisting two other students in the course with their assignments. In the course he exhibited determination, motivation, empathy, and a strong work ethic. I am certain that these qualities will ensure his success as an international student."

You might be interested in reading an actual letter of reference.

Letter of reference for Rachelle M.

Ms. M. was a student of mine from January to May 2018 in a small fourth year seminar course titled *The Politics of Aging* (POLS 4635). Her grades for the individual assignments in the course are shown below.

Diary #1	Article review	Diary #2	Proposal	Diary #3	Diary #4	Paper	Participation	Final %	Final
[5]	[20]	[5]	[5]	[5]	[5]	[40]	[15]		
Jan. 20	Jan. 27	Feb. 3	Feb. 10	Mar. 3	Mar. 16	Apr. 18	On-going		
4.7	16	3.9	3.5	4.5	4.7	36	13.5	87	A

She was a serious, engaged, motivated, organized, and pleasant student. In fact, I hired her on very short notice as a research assistant for two months to help me with editing a manuscript. Her work as my assistant was exemplary, notwithstanding tight deadlines.

Both as a student and as a research assistant, Ms. M. understood what was expected and delivered more. She was a high performing individual and student who I expect will make considerable contributions in the years to come in her field of study and work.

We have kept in touch after she graduated with her BA. She wisely decided to work – at a large private-sector health insurance company – for a year before beginning international studies at the graduate level in Britain. I am delighted that she has decided to pursue a MA in public policy, with a focus on healthcare, at your university. She demonstrated a true passion in the course I taught for policy analysis especially on healthcare topics. Her major paper in the course, for which she earned a grade of 90 per cent, was on healthcare for Inuit Peoples in Canada's Arctic region.

I have no hesitation in highly recommending her for both graduate studies and for international studies. In addition to being an exemplary student, Ms. M. is also a highly ethical individual with first-rate interpersonal skills. I have no doubt she will adjust without undue problems to her new environment in Britain and her colleagues at your university. Indeed, any graduate programme will find her a wonderful addition to the student body.

Do not hesitate to contact me via email or telephone if you believe that I might be of additional assistance regarding the application from Ms. M.

Cordially,
Thomas R. Klassen, PhD
Professor

Think about the recommendation letters that you wish your professors will write for you. You can help them write these by making sure to present them with the right information. This is especially the case if you have accomplishments since you completed the course that the professor taught. Be sure to stress these when you ask for a recommendation.

> **TIP 2.4** If you've been out of school for several years, you may have trouble finding people to write letters of reference for you. The best strategy is to ask professors or teachers, even if you think they will not remember you. Instructors are required to keep records of past students and are always happy to hear from someone they taught a long time ago. Also, you might be surprised that the teacher or professor, in fact, does remember you!

Sample of scholarly or creative work you have done

Often for international study applications you are asked to include a sample of your work. This can be an essay, a lab report, or if you are applying for a programme in the fine or creative arts, a drawing or a video of a performance. Give some thought about what to include.

Of course you want to send your best quality work. In addition, it should be something you wrote or created very recently, not several years ago.

It is quite fine to send an assignment that has comments on it from your professor or grader. Alternatively, it is also acceptable to send a new version of an assignment; that is, one that has corrections made from the original. In either case, you must be sure there is a cover page to the assignment including the date submitted to the professor, the course it was written for, the name of the department or university, and your name. You can also include a copy of the guidelines or instructions for the assignment, so the readers can see what you were asked to write.

If you've not been in school for a few years, you can send a copy of a document or presentation you prepared in your workplace. Just be sure to clearly state the sections or parts that you wrote/contributed. Obtain approval from your employer if the document or project was an internal one or is not to be shared outside of the workplace.

Transcript(s)

Nearly all applications require you to submit your transcript (the official record of your academic performance to-date). In some cases this is easy to obtain. In other cases less so, especially if you need to have the document translated or notarized.

Assume that obtaining and forwarding your transcript will take longer than you possibly thought it might, so start early in getting this done.

Results from standardized academic and language tests

If you are applying to start a degree abroad whether undergraduate (BA or BSc), a graduate (MA, MSc, MBA), or a doctorate (PhD) you will very likely have to write one or more standardized exams. There are many of these including the SAT (widely used for college admissions in the US), the GRE (Graduate Record Examination), and the GMAT (Graduate Management Admissions Test) for graduate studies.

In addition, you may have to write language specific tests to demonstrate your proficiency. If you are applying to international study programmes taught in English you almost certainly will need to write a standardized language test such as the IELTS (International English Language Testing System) or the TOEFL (Test of English as a Foreign Language) if you have not studied in English. Chapter 4 shows you how to do your very best on these tests including reducing stress, and having strategies for different kinds of tests.

There is planning required to write these tests. You may only be able to write them a few times a year in your home city. You also need to pay for each test you write. Many students write a test twice, as the second time usually ends up with a higher score. It makes sense to start early.

Résumé

The application form for your international education may require you to submit your résumé. Even if that is not a requirement, you can include a strong résumé as it will increase your odds of being admitted as the selection committee has more information about you. A résumé is a summary of your past accomplishments and if included in your application will avoid you having to explain your past achievements in your statement of interest. Chapter 7 shows you how to have a résumé that will wow them.[3]

Contacting the institution

As you prepare your application it is certain that you will have some questions about how to proceed. Consequently you'll need to contact the university or college you are applying to. There's a particular way to do this.

First, only contact the institution once you've already made a concerted effort to find the information yourself online, or in other ways such as talking to friends. You will be surprised at how much you can discover on your own.

Second, find the right person or office to submit your question to. Universities are large and bureaucratic organizations with different offices that handle admissions, financial aid, housing, and so forth.

Third, use email as your first option rather than calling on the telephone. Email gives the person on the other end time to find the information and respond. Email also means there is a record of your question and the reply.

Fourth, formulate your questions clearly. Vague questions will elicit vague and unhelpful replies. You could write: "I'm unsure of the deadline for submitting my language test results for my application. Can you help me?" A better question is: "On your website www.xxx.xxx the deadline for submitting language test result is May 15, but on your website www.xxx.yyy the date is shown as July 15. Could you please confirm for me which is the correct date: May 15 or July 15? I am applying from China as an international student for the Bachelor of Administrative Studies programme that begins in January 2020."

Fifth, use your best judgement. Suppose, the application asks for "three letters of recommendation, two of which should be from professors/teachers." You plan to ask three teachers to write letters on your behalf as you cannot find a non-teacher and have not worked. You are unsure if this is acceptable. Rather than spending time explaining this predicament to people in a university thousands of kilometers away, just proceed with what you think is best. Yes, ask three teachers to write you the letters! If you are uneasy about being proactive in this way, you can include a short note in the application stating why you did so.

Sixth, the best advice is not to wait until the deadline to try to get answers to your questions. This is because responses may not be immediate, and because you may be referred to a different office or person. The answer may require you to ask a follow-up question.

Government regulations

If you have not already, now is the time to learn about government regulations that will apply to you, such as a student visa and health insurance. The university that has accepted you will help, but the bulk of the work falls to you.

Don't lose heart! It will all come together!

Responding to being accepted

After waiting far too long, at last you've heard back and have been accepted to start your international studies. The first thing is to celebrate your achievement! Be pleased with yourself. And be sure to thank all those who helped and supported you.

If you've applied to several programmes or institutions, then you are wise to wait until all have responded. You may feel under pressure to accept the first offer, especially if that is your preferred choice. But, it is best to wait. You can write to the institution and explain that you need a couple more weeks to decide. Don't feel pressured. You will not be denied acceptance that is already granted if you request additional time to make a decision, no matter what the letter of acceptance states.

Obviously the university and programme that has accepted you would like you to accept immediately. This makes things easier for the staff who are juggling a waiting list of others who would like to attend. But your needs come first, and universities know this is a big decision for you especially as an international applicant.

You may find that as you receive other offers that your initial preference changes. Perhaps you have been offered a scholarship at one institution, but not another. Or you're feeling differently now that some months have passed since your application.

Even better, you can use the acceptance from one institution to negotiate a more generous funding package from another. This is how it works. You've been accepted by several institutions or programmes, each acceptance letter being slightly different. Perhaps more scholarship funds from one university, but lower tuition or accommodation costs at another.

If you are a graduate student you may have been offered a research or teaching assistantship in one programme, but not another. Or one of the colleges you've been accepted to is much closer to your home country or city, while the other is much further and therefore will entail higher costs to attend. Or, one college is a large urban setting where housing and living costs are high, while the other is in a locale with much lower living costs.

Decide the place you would most like to attend after having reviewed all the replies from all your applications. Write to the office or person from whom you've received the letter of admission and explain that "I would love to attend your programme, but I have also been accepted by [insert name of university] which has offered me [insert details]. As an international student I will have to bear significant costs. I wonder if you might be able to review the funding aspects of the offer that you sent me?"

The worst outcome is that you will be told "Sorry, we cannot change the offer." But, in a surprisingly number of cases some extra money or new arrangement will be offered. This is because, having offered you a place, the university does very much wish for you to attend. You are ranked higher than other students who would take your place if you do not attend. As such, there is every incentive for the university to make sure you say "Yes, I accept!"

Housing

After officially accepting an offer, the next task is to decide on housing in your new city and country. From our experience, feeling comfortable in the lodging arrangements is essential to flourishing while studying abroad.

In some cases, the university you will attend has offered you a place in a dormitory or student residence in its letter of acceptance. If so, there is relatively little for you to do, if that is the type of housing that you wish. The university will provide you with the options that are available and you select that which suits you best.

Alternatively, you need to find your own housing, if you prefer to do so. In this case, there are decisions you need to make in regard to the location and the type of accommodation.

Our general advice is to opt for housing – either on-campus or off – that places you in close proximity to others. In other words, a dormitory or student residence, or a shared house or apartment. Many students prefer to be on campus or very near, as this reduces transportation costs and time.

As you decide, be sure to listen to the voices of others: your friends and family. Conducting research on the experience of students similar to yourself will also aid in you securing the best place to live.

Notes

1 See www.timeshighereducation.com/student/best-universities/
   international-student-table-2018-top-200-universities
2 See www.rotary.org/en/our-programs/scholarships
3 In many cases, your application to study abroad will, to
   some extent, involve others in your family. A useful guide if
   applying to the US is Jennifer Ann Aquino's *The International
   Family Guide to US University Admissions* (Chichester: John
   Wiley, 2017).

CHAPTER 3

Adjusting to your new environment

Experience, travel – these are an education in themselves.

Euripides

Introduction

In this chapter we show you how to succeed in the first few days, weeks, and months of your life as an international student. After doing all the work to apply to study abroad and finally being admitted, you're at last ready to study, learn, and have fun in your new home.

Things will not always be easy and you'll be pushed to be your best. But the fun and learning will be more wonderful than you expected. Let the pages that follow help you.

When I decided to study for my bachelor's degree in the UK I was hoping to improve my English as well as have a great time. What I experienced was so much more!

I got used to the lectures in English quickly – once I got a hang of the terminology, and I even learned to understand one of my Scottish professors who had a very strong accent.

I studied in Cambridge, which has a high percentage of students, making the city lively and vibrant during the day, as well as at night. I spent a lot of time travelling around the UK as well, which was fairly easy with trains. This gave me the opportunity to learn more about the cultural differences between my home country and the UK.

Studying abroad helped me develop both on a professional and personal level.

The ability to discuss ideas and perceptions with people from all over the world, being pushed out of my comfort zone and at the same time getting a good education did not only prepare me for a professional career, but also gave me a broader understanding of how the world works. During my time studying abroad I met people from various countries with whom I still keep in touch. I now have the possibility of travelling all over the world and always have a local with me who can show me around!

Daniel B. Enzinger

Finding the right courses

Before you even arrive at your new home you may have to enrol online for courses or programmes, and undertake other administrative tasks. Online your host institution may advertise a range of courses that you can enrol in, many of which look attractive. However, once actually ready to sign up, you may discover that you're not eligible for all or that priority is given to local students or that you don't have the required prerequisites.

If you've arrived to study for an entire programme, you may find that the information online is not quite accurate. You may be admitted into your preferred programme of studies, but may be obliged to complete additional courses or other preparations. Programmes evolve and you will need to be flexible.

Rather than being frustrated, start with the understanding that you will need to be creative in selecting programmes and courses, and that you may find yourself taking courses that you had never imagined you would. That's all OK and part of the experience.

If you are an exchange student you may have trouble meeting the requirements of your home institution with respect to courses. Again our advice is to be flexible. Enrol in the courses that seem the most interesting. Be sure to keep copies of your course syllabi and assignments completed. Once you return to your home university, you can begin the process of getting the appropriate credit and recognition for what you've learned.

One strategy is to sign up for as many courses as possible at the start of the term, and then drop them or shop around for those you really like.

Studying abroad may also limit your access to resources, such as hardcopy books and magazines in your native language. The libraries in your high school, or home institution (if you are an exchange student) may have had tens of thousands of books in your language. Your study abroad library may have much fewer. Again, creativity is the key, especially when using the internet.

Of course, sometimes the situation may be the reverse. Your home university may have had a limited selection of materials, while your study away university has many times that. If that is the case, then do take advantage of the bounty!

First days in your new country

The first few days will be exciting, overwhelming, and likely a time you will remember for the rest of your life. Be prepared to feel out of place. Everything may be new, and even different from what you imagined.[1]

It would be wonderful if these days go by smoothly and that nothing has been lost or forgotten; and that all the arrangements you made some time ago work out perfectly. But that will not be the case. Some aspects of your first days will not go as planned.

Here's how to avoid disasters and reduce the inevitable snags:

1. Make sure you're well rested before departing from your home. You may be busy partying, saying goodbye, shopping, and packing, but make sure to fit in good food and enough sleep. This will prevent you from getting sick upon arrival in your new home.

2.   Pack everything you will need for the first few days in your carry-on luggage. This way, if you are separated from your luggage, you will still have everything you need. In any case, make sure to pack essential items (medication, contact lenses, cosmetics, and so forth) in your carry-on. You want to make certain these remain with you at all times.

3.   Pack some of your favourite foods. You may very well be able to buy these in your new location, but perhaps not during the first days. Have your comfort food close at hand.

4.   Confirm arrangements before your departure. Don't assume that those expecting you (at your new accommodation and other places) will remember that you are arriving at a particular date and time.

5.   Do some research to learn if there will be free Wi-Fi at the airport once you arrive. Is there a particular social media platform what most people use in your new locale? What will the weather be like (which you need to know to pack your carry-on bag)?

6.   Inform your financial institution and credit card companies that you will be moving to your new location. Make certain that your credit card(s) will not be blocked due to unusual transactions. Increase your credit limit, if possible, to take into account that you may have initial expenditures.

7.   Bring some cash with you. Your credit cards may not be accepted in all shops, and you will need cash for some transactions (such as deposits). You don't want to carry too much money on you, but at the same time you don't what to run out.

For the first few days, keep your expectations modest. You may not have time to see much of what you want to as you will be busy with various necessary, but unexciting, tasks such as: opening a bank account (be sure you check what documents you need to bring); finalizing accommodation arrangements; getting a phone and/or phone services (again, check before you depart as to what is needed). You may need to take some considerable time to obtain documents from the local government and university that will allow you to remain in the country.

You will be eager to spend time sightseeing, or at beaches, or art galleries, or clubs, but during the first few days you are better off learning where the nearest pharmacy or drug store is located, and where to find essential items. The fun stuff will be even more fun after you've got yourself more organized.

TIP 3.1   You may be tempted to sample the local food during the first days in your new home. But, unless you are confident your body is used to the cuisine, wait for a while to avoid the possibility of getting ill.

The first weeks on campus

If you are coming to international studies after having completed a year or more of studies in your home country, you will feel like you are back in the first year again. Remember the first few weeks of high school or university? How lost you often were? How confusing the names and acronyms seemed? How everything took three times as long? You will feel all these feelings again when studying abroad.

If your international studies are straight from high school, then you are in for even more running around and getting lost. Universities are usually much bigger than high schools, and initially much more confusing.

Be sure to attend all the orientation events that have been organized for you. More than that, seek out other orientation occasions such as on how to use the library. If your university has mentors or buddies, be certain to spend time with them. Fairly quickly you'll feel more comfortable, make friends, and learn to navigate the campus and the institution. The key is to expect a period of bewilderment.

What will take more adjustment time is deciphering the expectations of your professors and classmates. Unless you are in a programme or course filled with other international students, such as in international MBA programme, you will in some ways feel like a duck out of water. You may be the only international student in a classroom. Your teacher and your classmates may not quite know what to make of you, and you may not know what to make of them!

It will be your task to take care of the situation, not your professor or fellow students.

I am in my second year of a PhD programme in Phoenix, Arizona. My first two months in the US were full of stress due to paperwork and uncertainties derived from being a foreigner. I had no friends, no family, no one to rely on. I had to figure out what to do myself. The only thing I could rely on was Google.

After settling in, the huge school workload overwhelmed me. There were many readings and assignments, and I had to struggle to finish the projects on time. I wondered whether my struggle was due to my limited language ability or just a demanding programme of studies.

What I like the most about my PhD programme is the relationship with professors. I currently work with five professors on five projects. They all have a different style, but are all very supportive and open-minded. I feel a lot more comfortable talking with professors in the US because the relationship is much more lateral than in my past degrees. One reason is the English language. I don't find it intimidating to talk with professors because English speakers do not use different expressions depending on the age or organizational rank of the listener, unlike my mother tongue, Korean.

Pursuing a PhD degree as an international student has been tough work, but also incredibly rewarding. I learn new things every day, including how to express myself professionally at conferences, meetings for projects, and even social events. However, it is also true that I sometimes tell myself that life sucks when I am stressed out with too much work!

Haneul Choi

Making friends

Making friends is crucial to having the time of your life as an international student. For some people making friends seems to require less effort than for others.

Here are seven techniques for making friends quickly and easily as an international student regardless of language and other barriers. Adapt them to your own circumstances and to who you are:

1. Smile. Nothing is as easy and simple.
2. Make an effort to learn the names of others and pronounce the names correctly.
3. Look for people with whom you have something in common: gender, age, appearance (such as clothing). Your classes are good places to initially make friends.
4. Expect friendships to take time to develop, and for deep friendships to take a long time. Be realistic.
5. Don't be needy or pushy. You may not always be aware that you are being needy or pushy in your dealings with others. It happens to everyone at some time.
6. Food is a great way to make friends as we all need to eat. Offer to cook something for people who you'd like to get to know better.
7. Be respectful of the local culture.

A frustration you are likely to experience is that many of your initial friends will be non-locals. That is, other international students. This may be infuriating as you came abroad to make friends with the locals, and learn a new language. For example, you moved to an English-speaking country with the express purpose of becoming more proficient. Yet, you are living and studying with a group of other people from all over the world, and have not one native-English speaking friend.

TIP 3.2 Bring small gifts from your home country. Nothing expensive, but something only available from your nation or region. Use these to express your thanks to people you meet abroad, or to those who have been kind to you.

As a result you're going to feel pressure to make English-speaking friends (or whatever the local language is). But the local students already have friends and don't seem to be in a hurry to make friends with you. What to do?

A poor strategy is to approach people and ask if they will help you practice or learn English. The vast majority of local students have no interest in helping you – or anyone – improve language skills. There's nothing in it for them. In the same way, would you want to be friends with someone solely to help that person learn a language?

Slow down. No one is going to be friends with you to help you improve your language proficiency. That's not friendship.

> **TIP 3.3**   People may have trouble pronouncing or spelling your name, or perhaps even understanding your accent. You can have simple business cards printed (usually for a very low cost using internet-based services) with your name and phone number. Maybe even an emoji or other happy sign. You can hand these out when the time seems right.

You might be tempted to find friends and trade skills: "You help me with my English and I'll help you with another language or skill." But that too is not real friendship. In some cases this kind of trade works, but not very often.

Look to make friends with people you have something in common with: whether it be in regard to your courses, or movies, music or art, or sports, or travel, or any other pastime. Some of these people will be locals and will over time effortlessly become your friends.

To make this happen, you may need to go outside of your comfort zone. If your comfort zone is talking to people in your dormitory who are all international students, then you need to extend this. The best way is to follow the seven suggestions above.

Bad times

There will be bad times and you will feel depressed at certain periods during your international study. That is to be expected.

You spent much time and maybe a lot of money, and overcame obstacles and resistance, to study abroad. You were hoping and expecting everything to fall into place. But it didn't, or least not a quickly as you hoped. Anger, sadness and depression are logical when that happens.

Maybe something got lost or broken, or the accommodation is not what you expected, or the weather is not pleasant, or friends are difficult to make. You may miss your family, friends, and classmates halfway around the world. The food may taste terrible and you cannot communicate easily with the people around you.

You may feel that you are being discriminated against because of the colour of your skin, your accent, or something else. Or you may be feeling physically unwell. And, your studies may be much more grueling than you ever dreamt with professors providing feedback that makes you question your abilities, or the grades you are earning are not even close to what you got back home.

Some of the above – and maybe all of it or more – will happen to you. Every minute will not be fun and every experience will not be fantastic. One of the reasons you've chosen to go abroad is to face difficulties and obstacles, learn a new perspective, prove yourself, and stretch yourself.[2] Some of the difficulties you will invariably face will decline in severity just by the passage of time.

The passage of time will take care of some things: the sun will shine, friendships will take hold, and you'll find or cook more tasty food. Other things may not improve much. A course that you don't like may not become better but rather more demanding. In this case, you need to persevere. The course will not last forever, only some more weeks or a few months. The course only takes up a few hours of your week. You can also share your dislike of the course with others, and talking about things can make you feel better.

But sometimes things don't seem to get better. You may continue to desperately miss your friends or family at home. Or you may continue to feel uncomfortable in your new home.

If you feel you've waited long enough and have tried to persevere, then the next step is to talk at length to others about what is happening to you: friends, family, advisers, and counsellors. Your university will likely have an international student centre, and will have a range of services and people on campus to help you with personal and study concerns. Be sure to visit the campus counselling services where you can speak to someone.

Trust the advice you're hearing from the people you are sharing your circumstances with. They do have your best interests at heart, and may have seen other students in similar situations. They may know you better than you imagine. In some cases, just being able to talk about your situation with a professional will make you feel better and add perspective.

Going back home is always an option and you must keep that in mind. It may be the wrong time in your life for international studies, or you are at the wrong place. That can happen and there is no shame if that occurs. For example, a relationship may have become important at home to you between the time you applied for international studies and the time you left to go abroad.

If, after careful reflection and consultation with others, you decide to return home be sure to follow the appropriate process. Don't pack your bags and go straight to the airport. Speak to the people you need to speak to at your university: at the dormitory or apartment, your professors, the staff at your department, or programme of study, and international student centre. Let everyone know that you are leaving. It may take a few extra days to get all this done (paperwork is never quick), but you will feel much better about yourself and avoid unnecessary problems and costs. By following the process you may be eligible for refunds and perhaps even salvage some course credits.

The great thing about international studies is that they are always available for you. If it does not work out this time, then it will next time. Perhaps you and a close friend will do it together. Perhaps for a different time period at another location.

To keep that option open is another reason to follow the bureaucratic process if you are leaving for home early, even if there is nothing that you would like more than to get out of there. Lastly, not bolting shows that you are a mature and resilient person who can extricate himself or herself from a tough situation.

Safety

International students are always placed in safe surroundings, and those responsible at the university abroad take safety very seriously. Most often you will have housing that is owned or managed by the university and be provided with, or need to provide proof that you have, health insurance.

In some cases you will be asked to attend a safety briefing at your new university. Be sure to attend, and be sure to ask questions!

On the other hand, by travelling away from home, you are deemed to be an adult and to have the skills and knowledge to ensure your safety. In many cases, this may be the first time you've lived away from home, travelled and lived on your own.

Safety includes:

1. Doing things in the daytime, such as shopping, until you are comfortable and knowledgeable in your new environment.
2. Not carrying or wearing expensive items (phones, jewellery and computers).
3. Staying with a crowd or friends, especially in unfamiliar situations or environments.
4. Knowing how to ask or call for help, and not hesitating to do so. Be sure to know the numbers to call for emergency responders.
5. Take action immediately if something feels wrong.

Doing research on your location before you depart will help you feel comfortable and safe. And, of course, once you arrive if at any time you feel insecure, be sure to report this to officials or others at your school. Many students create a network of support that operates in the case of an emergency. Arrange regular times during the week to call home or a friend.

Lastly, trust yourself. Ignore those who tell you "This is OK in my country" when it is something you don't agree with or are uncomfortable with.

Being popular/unpopular

As an international student you're likely going to be very popular at times, and then very unpopular at other times.[3] Being popular – because of your skin colour, eye colour, accent, dress or cosmetics, or whatever is fun. Enjoy it! You may be seen as exotic. You may be told how cute your accent is or how fabulous you look.

But be prepared for the opposite to also occur: to be shunned or discriminated against because of your skin colour, dress, or accent. That will hurt. You may not be used to being part of the minority or being seen as different in a negative way.

Fortunately, university campuses are the most open and accepting places on the planet. You'll not find much prejudice or intolerance there. However, when you travel outside of your institution, things may be different.

Try to remember that whether people are being extra nice to you, or the opposite, their behaviour is solely based on superficial characteristics that they can see about you: skin colour, or dress. They don't know you. So, best not to take their comments or actions seriously at all.

Remain cordial and calm, even if you might be seething inside. Don't respond even if you feel slighted or insulted.

Respect the local culture

In your new home you will want to fit in, perhaps not all the time, but most of the time. Being an outsider is fun and healthy for a while, but not for too long.

You may need to make some changes to what you wear and how you dress. If no one else is wearing shorts, you might not want to be the only one. If people take their shoes off indoors, then you must as well. If locals are not taking photos of a particular locale, then you shouldn't either.

The advice here is not that you should act and dress like a local, but rather that what was acceptable and cool back home might be perceived differently in your new environment. You are a guest both at your university and in the larger society. Guests act in a particular way regardless of how they might feel.

Not only are you a guest, but you're also an ambassador. You represent your home city and country. More so, you may represent an entire culture and way of life. You may be the first person your new colleagues and friends have ever met from your home locale.

Sharing your experience

Now you're all settled, making friends, learning lots, and having the time of your life. If you have free time, consider sharing your experience. You can create a blog or a website, in addition to other social media such as Facebook. For sure you've taken some awesome photos of amazing sites, found out-of-the-way clubs, and tasted some delicious meals.

Creating your own website using a free platform is a wonderful way to let others know what you're up to. A personal website also lets you develop social media skills that will be important as time to graduate comes around (see Chapters 6 and 9).

But be sure not to post close-up photos of people unless you have their express permission and they understand on what social media platform their image will be posted. Be sure to show the photos you plan to post, rather than asking general permission to post photos. Look at Chapter 9 to see how to use social media to your advantage, and how to avoid problems.

For parents: As your child studies abroad, you'll need to take steps to stay connected and share experiences from your home. Keeping and strengthening connections with your child can be done using Skype, Zoom, Snapchat, or making a Facebook event page. Regularly sharing photos, videos, and stories of people, celebrations and happenings back home can be essential to making the study abroad experience a successful one for your child.

Employment

Once settled and having fun, and learning lots, you might be tempted to seek part-time employment. Maybe for the experience, the extra spending money, or just because an interesting employment offer has been made to you.

In many cases you cannot legally work or can do so only under very specific conditions (such as on campus and for a maximum number of hours a week). Check to see what the rules are both from your university, any scholarships you might have, and from the local government.

Our general advice is to not work unless you are required to do so as part of your educational programme. Being an international student is likely to keep you pretty occupied and with your spare time there is lots to explore.

However, if you are offered an internship, cooperative education experience, or education placement, feel free to accept it if permitted by the university and local government; but only if you can manage the additional commitment. Of course, sometimes the placement is part of a course or programme, in which case you have no choice but to participate.

You may also find yourself being offered – or perhaps feeling pressured – to accept "under-the-table" employment. That is being paid in cash and not being formally registered as an employee. Perhaps in a job in the service industry, or perhaps as a language tutor or something else.

If this occurs just say "no!" (to yourself or others). Accepting this type of illegal work places you in jeopardy as you have little recourse if something happens, such as not being paid or being injured at your place of employment. You also face the possibility of deportation and other sanctions.

If you find that money is a concern, then the first step is to talk to the international student office (or equivalent) at your university to seek advice.

Our last word concerns volunteer opportunities that might arise. It is quite acceptable to take advantage of volunteer employment: helping out on campus, or friends, or at a community event. These do not demand the same type of commitment as an employment contract. With volunteer work you can say "Sorry, I am busy this week due to a big test that is coming up."

You will not be paid for volunteer work, but it is a marvelous way to make new friends, learn about your new home, and can be beneficial when you are drafting your résumé as employers value volunteer experience and the skills you have gained through it.

Mobilize your professors

Professors can be difficult to interact with at the best of times. As an international student you may face even more complications than you are used to in your own country. Here's advice that will ease your dealings with professors, teaching assistants, lab instructors, librarians, and others.

First, during the initial meeting of a course or tutorial at the start of the semester, introduce yourself briefly to the instructor before or after class. This is what you can say: "My name is Theresa Tang.

I'm an international student from Beijing, China, starting my first year of university education. I arrived last week in your country and plan to complete a four year degree in economics."

If there is no opportunity to catch the attention of a professor or teaching assistant before or after class, go and visit the professor during office hours. However, wait until the third week of classes to do this, as typically office hours are busy for the first couple of weeks of the term with students facing more difficult situations than yours.

By briefly introducing yourself to your professors and other instructors, they will understand that you may not be used to the cultural norms of the classroom, and may have some language barriers. Note that you've not said any of this, but possibly your accent may have communicated some of that.

The key is to state facts in a few sentences. If in the future you need to have a longer conversation with an instructor, then you've already established contact and the professor will remember you.

Don't say things like "My English is not very good, and I'm not sure I have the required background for this course. I'm anxious about your class and reading the textbook. I'm sure I will do badly." The initial conversation with your professor is not for you to explain your situation, signal that you may be a problem student, or share your feelings.

Second, if you are very uncomfortable introducing yourself to instructors in person, you can do so over email. This is not as effective as a brief in-person chat, but better than doing nothing. In Chapter 5 we show you how to make oral presentations (like introductions) much less stressful.

Third, feel free to meet with the instructor during office hours as the course progresses. You may be surprised to learn how very few students go to the professor's office after the first two weeks. Don't be shy. There is everything to be gained from being proactive.

However, only meet with your instructor one-on-one when you have a substantive question or problem. Is there something you failed to grasp in the last lecture, lab, or reading? Is there something that your professor can aid you with? Don't go there to complain how hard the course is, how poorly you did in the last test, how long the required readings are, how rushed the laboratory work feels to you, or about your language skills. These are not topics to discuss with a professor. You can talk about these topics with classmates, friends, and family.

If you find yourself struggling in a course, and you likely will at some point, approach the professor with your own suggestions and seek ideas from him or her. Ask if you might audio or even video tape the lectures so you can play these back. Are there past tests that can be made available for you to review?

Ask the professor for other resources. Are there other textbooks that he or she can recommend to supplement the one you are using? Could the professor review an assignment with you one more time? Are there other assignments the professor can suggest for you?

> **TIP 3.4**   Don't ask a professor if you can re-do an assignment or re-write a test. Nothing demonstrates a lack of maturity more than a student saying "Is there anything I can do improve grades I've already earned?"

Don't ask for preferential treatment because you are an international student. That's not how university works. Professors will not change how they are teaching a course because of what you think, need, or want. You have to adjust to what is being taught and how.

Remember that the professor wants you to do the best possible work. To perform at your best. But this is a partnership in which you do most of the work. After all, the professor already knows the material.

Often some of the adjustment that international students have to make is not so much related to the course material. After all, biology, economics, or most other subjects are the same whether taught in country A or country B.

Rather the adjustment is related to the informal elements of classroom life. Things that are not written down. Such as, is it acceptable to ever miss any classes? Is it acceptable to interrupt a professor if you need a clarification during a lecture? Are the deadlines firm or flexible? Will the material from optional reading be on the exam? And much more. Even, how do I address my instructor: As Professor Sanders? Or Dr Sanders? Or Mr Sanders? Or Mr Michael Sanders? Or Professor? Or Sir?

There is no way to learn these informal rules without being in the environment. So for the first few weeks and months of your international studies you will be an investigator, paying close attention to how others act around you. Don't assume that how things worked at home is how they will work in your new home!

Plagiarism

Many students, not only international students, struggle with plagiarism. However, international students struggle more because what is seen as plagiarism by teachers and professors varies from country to country.

Plagiarism is using someone else's writing without giving proper credit. In other words, to present someone else's writing as your own. Doing so is serious, even if you did so unintentionally. The best thing is to always cite the sources from which you obtained facts, ideas, or entire phrases, sentences, and paragraphs.

The general rule is that you cannot copy and paste without acknowledging the original source and placing quotation marks around the words you copied and pasted.

We have more to say about this in Chapter 4, but the general advice is to check your new university's website for guidelines and tutorials, as well as any information related to the course. And, don't hesitate to meet with your instructor or grader before submitting an assignment to review your understanding of plagiarism.

On your way

The above might seem like a long list of do's and don'ts, but that's not the case. Most things will fall into place with flexibility, patience, and hard work on your part.[4]

Trust us, after the first few months, everything will be going smoothly. Indeed, we hope you will look back fondly on how you rose to meet all the challenges as you began your studies abroad.

Notes

1   There is much that has been written about visiting foreign lands, from Homer's *Iliad* to Marco Polo, not to mention numerous movies. If you are looking for recent novels, check out *The Foreign Student* by Susan Choi (1998) and *The Foreign Student* by Philippe Labro (1988). More books are listed at http://flavorwire.com/560227/25-excellent-novels-about-americans-abroad/view-all and www.isepstudyabroad.org/articles/363. Movies that capture studying and travelling abroad include: *L'Auberge Espagnole* (2002), *Lost in Translation* (2003), and *Best Exotic Marigold Hotel* (2011).

2   If you are living or travelling in a place not as wealthy as your home country, you might feel discomfort or confusion in how to behave. Look at Anu Taranath, *Beyond Guilt Trips: Mindful Travel in an Unequal World* (Toronto: Between the Lines Press, 2019).

3   Maya Van Wagenen, a middle school student, writes about her efforts to be popular in a new environment in the insightful and entertaining *Popular: Vintage Wisdom for a Modern Geek* (New York: Vantage/Penguin Books, 2014).

4   If you're interested in a scholarly perspective on the experience of international students, check out Krishna Bista, ed. *Global Perspectives on International Student Experiences in Higher Education: Tensions and Issues* (New York: Routledge, 2019).

Essential classroom skills (I)

Exams and essays

*Great things are not done by impulse, but by a series
of small things brought together.*

Vincent van Gogh

Introduction

You may be starting your study abroad as an experienced university student, perhaps one who has completed a degree already, or you've just graduated from high school. Whichever the case, studying abroad will be both more difficult and more fun than you expected.

This chapter will help you to perform strongly on exams, tests, essays, and reports in your new environment. As an international student, perhaps one learning in a language that is not your mother tongue, you confront unique obstacles in doing your best on exams and essays.

Exams

As you already know, performing well on exams is essential to succeed in school. However, mastering exams and tests is also crucial if you wish to get ahead in the workplace after completing your studies.

It is common for job applications to involve written tests. In fact, for many jobs – in both the public and private sector – candidates must pass various exams before they're offered an interview. The interview itself is an exam: on what you've learned and how well you can organize and present your thoughts and ideas. Doing well in an interview is difficult if you can't recall important information, respond to unexpected questions, or are just stressed out.

Many professionals, such as lawyers, accountants, engineers, and financial advisers, must write qualifying and competency exams. After you complete your bachelor's degree, you might decide to continue your studies, perhaps taking an MBA or other master's degree. Many of these programmes require candidates to pass an entrance exam, such as the GMAT (for business school), or GRE (for graduate school).

Finally, you'll face many real-life tests each and every day at work. For instance, your boss may ask you to describe, right now, the underlying problems of your latest project or account. Or a client may call and ask you to explain why you made recommendations last year. If you cannot respond to their questions, they'll take their business elsewhere.

Reducing anxiety

Let's face it – exams are stressful. If you're not anxious about them, pinch yourself, because you're probably dead.

The words "exam" and "test" strike terror in the hearts of many students. A professor merely needs to whisper "This might be on the test" to get the full attention of a lecture hall of hundreds of students. You're never going to eliminate exam or performance-related anxiety, either at school or at work, but you can reduce it. It makes sense to begin this process while you're still in school and to carry that lower anxiety into the workforce.

You may be pleasantly surprised how much better you perform on exams when your anxiety level is lower. This is especially true for international students who are adjusting to a new school and environment.

In order of importance, here are the six effective ways of decreasing exam anxiety:

1. Know your stuff. Understand the material on which you are being tested. In particular, understand the key ideas or themes in a course and how the facts fit into them.
2. Don't memorize: make understanding your goal. Memorization is one of the worst ways to organize data. Good exams don't assess your capacity to memorize; rather they determine how well you understand the material. You may discover that your anxiety level drops once you no longer have to memorize so much.
3. Don't cram at the last minute. We know, we know – it worked in high school, right? Well, it won't work as well, or at all, at university.
4. If you simply must cram, do it intelligently. Just pack your short-term memory with basic facts, names, and dates, but don't try to learn the key concepts or ideas at the last minute.
5. Control excessive stress, don't try to eliminate it. Divide your exam preparation into smaller steps. When it all seems overwhelming, get some exercise, watch a movie, or go out for an evening.
6. Put things in perspective. An exam is not a life-or-death situation. Believe it or not, many, many people have failed exams and gone on to brilliant careers.

Preparing for a big exam

Not all exams are big exams. Worrying about small tests or spending hours preparing for an exam in an easy course is a waste of time. For the big scary exams it's good to have a personal strategy.

Here's a strategy that works for many international students and that can be customized to suit your circumstances:

• Reduce the pressure on yourself. Concentrate on doing as well as you can rather than aiming for a specific grade. You cannot change the fact that you're an international student and may face particular barriers on the exam.

- Forget about the future. In particular, forget about the impact that the exam might have on your future. Concentrate on the here and now.
- Focus. Live and breathe exam preparation rather than the exam itself. Exam preparation is not scary.
- Complain like crazy. Tell all your friends that you are preparing for a big exam and that you cannot have a social life (or any life to speak of) until it's over. They'll take the hint and leave you alone, which will allow you to get on with preparing for the exam.
- Organize all your study materials and surroundings. This can be a formal ritual to help you start working. But don't let the organizing take over from the studying.
- Take breaks whether you need them or not. Studying is an open-ended activity. It stops only when the exam itself begins. This means that you need to schedule regular breaks while studying.
- Identify major gaps in your knowledge early in the preparation process. Don't wait until the last minute to discover that you don't understand important elements.
- Rewrite your notes. Reading over your notes is not an effective way to prepare for a test. If you rewrite your notes more of the ideas and information will stick, and you will make connections not spotted before. This is exceptionally valuable if you are studying in a language that is new to you.
- Get a good night's sleep. On the evening before the exam, tell yourself that you've done all you can. At this point, sleeping well is the best thing you can do for yourself, so you can focus all your energy on the exam itself.

Here are six tips to help you do well on exam day:

1. Make sure you've got what you need, including extra pens and pencils.
2. Get to the examination room early. As an international student you may think you know where the exam is and what the arrangements are (such as identification you need to bring), but get there early just in case.
3. When you open up the exam, relax and take the time to read it all. Don't start writing immediately.

4.   Pay attention to the marking scheme. You want to identify which questions are worth the most marks and ensure that you don't spend too long on any one area.
5.   Be strategic. For example, set your sights on finishing the entire exam, rather than getting a perfect mark.
6.   Focus on the questions. Read them carefully. Read them at least twice. Then read them again.

Strategies for multiple-choice exams

Many international students prefer multiple-choice questions on exams to essay questions. With multiple-choice exams the correct answer is in front of you; all you need to do is identify it. In addition, you don't need to write sentences and paragraphs in a language that you may not be fluent in, or meet expectations of graders that you may not fully understand.

But multiple choice exams can still be very tricky, and preparing for them is difficult. Multiple-choice exams play with technicalities, analogies, and comparisons that take time to decipher (but you usually don't have enough time). This is even harder in a language that may not be your native tongue.

It important to understand why people do badly on multiple-choice exams: they read the questions too quickly, get stuck on one or two early on, and pace themselves poorly.

Here's a seven-step strategy to help you with multiple-choice exams:

1.   Do all the easy questions first. This will make you feel good and will build your confidence, since you'll get most of them right. Spending too much time on the hard questions may prevent you from answering all the easy ones.
2.   Read the difficult questions carefully. Circle the key words. Try to come up with the answer before looking at the choices and perhaps becoming confused.
3.   Then check the choices. They often trigger an answer. For example, if you know that three answers are incorrect, the remaining one must be right.

4. If you don't know the answer, take your best guess and quickly move on. Plugging away at one question is a poor strategy in a multiple-choice exam. If marks are deducted for errors, leave the question blank and move on.
5. Check the questions for double negatives that make the right answer a positive. For example, a double negative such as "not unnecessary" translates to "necessary," and "not impossible" means "possible."
6. Review and review again, if you have time. If you finish early, keep going over the questions. You are guaranteed to find at least one that you answered incorrectly.
7. Do not change answers that are guesses. This is a waste of time.

Strategies for exams with short answer and essay questions

Written exams can consist of short answer questions and essay questions. Short answers are usually easier to write than essays because they tend to test factual recall and can usually be written in point form. International students prefer these.

Essays are more difficult because they assess your ability, not only to analyse course material, but also to synthesize it in meaningful ways. The advantage of an essay exam is that it puts the ball firmly in your court. You decide how best to answer the question to show off your understanding of the course materials. In other words, you can be creative in answering questions, as recalling facts is not the major objective of such questions.

Many of the strategies for a written exam are the same as for a multiple-choice exam. You need to read the questions carefully, divide your time appropriately in terms of their worth, and pace yourself.

In addition, you should spend at least 20 per cent of your time creating an outline for each answer. This time is well spent, since it allows you to compose your essay quickly and to ensure that it is clearly organized.

If you don't manage to finish an essay, the outline will show your marker that you've mastered the course material, understood the question and knew how to answer it, but ran out of time. Markers in most universities will grade a good outline almost as generously as they would a full essay.

To do well on essay exams, you need to:

- comprehend the theories and key ideas of the course;
- have strong writing skills (which can be a particular problem for international students, and are discussed later in this chapter); and
- understand and respond to the question!

Why the exclamation mark? Consider this awful truth – students often fail essay exams because they don't pay enough attention to the precise language and intent of the question. If you don't answer the question, it doesn't matter how much you know, or how much you write, or how much you understand. Unless you have a very kind professor, you will earn a low grade.

If you misread a multiple-choice question, you'll lose only a few marks. But if you misread an essay question on a four-question exam, the best mark that you can possibly achieve is 75 per cent. And only if you answer the remaining three questions perfectly. That's why it's so important to read essay exam questions carefully. The rule of thumb is to spend at least ten minutes breaking down the question and ensuring that you've understood it before beginning to write.

Key words in exam questions

Understanding the key words in exam questions is the key (pardon the pun) to answer the question. Sometimes international students are unclear about what is being asked when specific terms appear on exam questions.

Here's a guide to help:

- To **trace** is to show the evolution of something from start to finish.
- To **outline** is to focus on the main components of something.

- To **illustrate** is to provide concrete examples to support an argument.
- To **explain** is to give the reasons for, or causes of, something.
- To **discuss** is to weigh the pros and cons of something.
- To **criticize** or **evaluate** is to assess the merit of something in considerable depth.
- To **interpret** is to find a deeper meaning or underlying pattern in something.
- To **review** is to go over an event or explanation so as to analyse it in a fresh way.
- To **compare** is to focus on the similarities, differences, and links between ideas or events.
- To **argue** is to give reasons for and against.
- To **assess** is to sift through arguments and evidence to build a case.

Essays

The most critical skill to learn in university is how to explain things. In other words, you must learn how to provide others with a convincing interpretation that explains a particular event, idea, problem, or development.

At some point during your university career, you will write at least one essay. If you applied to become an international student you've almost certainly had to write a statement to the answer: "Why should I be accepted?" See Chapter 2 for the importance of these statements in applications to colleges, and for financial aid.

After you graduate, or even before, you will need to write job applications. See Chapter 7 for how to write a résumé and a cover letter. These are essays ("Why I should be hired") as are statements of interest for applications to university programmes.

Essay writing is all about explaining things to others, and more specifically about learning how to do this well. It doesn't matter whether the subject is Byzantine architecture, commodity investments, climate change, a novel, or why you should be hired for a job.[1] The skills are the same regardless of the topic of your essay.

Use your essays to generate concise, well-grounded, and interesting explanations and arguments. Sometimes settling on an essay topic can be difficult, especially if your professor or teaching assistant lets you choose your own. You can solve this problem – as have many other international students – by selecting a topic that relates to your home country. After all, you already have a wealth of knowledge!

Some particularly ambitious international students select a topic related to their new home. After all, this will require learning something new, about something that may have struck you as fascinating about your new environment.

Writing essays, especially good ones, is work, but it's enjoyable if it relates to your interests. It's not enough to be interested in a subject. You need to approach it in a rigorous way. Academic writing, and especially scientific writing, is the most objective kind of prose.

The academic writer has a particular obligation to communicate information that is as precise, unbiased, and correct as possible. Hyperbole and overly dramatic wording is not part of good academic writing, because it detracts from efficiency of communication and prevents clear communication.

Students sometimes complain that professors are "too picky" or "should have known" what was meant in an essay. But academic writing is all about precision and clarity. Stylistic and grammatical errors, and faulty logic, are penalized because bad writing obscures meaning and impedes effective communication.

Unsupported arguments are questioned, not because your professor necessarily disagrees with you, but because such writing is unscholarly. But more than that, your professors want to make certain you have the writing skills that will function to your advantage after graduation.

In the professional world, you'll be expected to back up every statement you make. If you have a tendency to make statements on the basis of emotion/intuition, your employers and colleagues will label you a loose cannon. The problem with loose cannons is that they're inaccurate and can even threaten the harmony of the ship. As a result, they tend to be dismissed or demoted to jobs where they can't do much damage.

A professor may give you some leeway if you muddle your argument, or provide insufficient evidence, or write with grammatical errors especially as an international student. This is as it should be. After all, university is a place to learn and that means making mistakes. However, you can bet that the person who pays your salary and relies on your expertise in very tangible ways won't cut you any slack at all.

Writing for the academic reader

Whenever you write, whatever you write, keep your audience in mind. Many students fall into the trap of trying to write for a particular instructor and waste time figuring out what will please him or her. Some students even go so far as pretending to support the ideas or theories that their teacher holds.

This is usually a misguided approach. It may work with one or two instructors, but it's a low-percentage strategy. It's far wiser to apply your energy to constructing an academically sound argument. In this way you'll gain the skills that will make you a better writer at the university level.

Every academic essay is expected to include the following qualities:

- **Completeness and comprehensiveness:** Academic writers must clearly locate their work within a body of knowledge, demonstrate how it contributes to that knowledge, and proceed from a statement of the problem to its resolution.
- **Order:** Academic writing presents material in a logical order. Difficult or problematic data are introduced carefully. Every section of the essay is structured clearly, and the transition between sections must demonstrate coherent development. The ideas and information in each paragraph are related to each other.
- **Accuracy:** Academic writers must provide accurate information. This means that they must check all their statements to ensure that they are not obscuring the data or jumping to false conclusions. If you are not sure about something, don't include it in your essay!
- **Impartiality:** Academic writing is impartial. Academic writers – whether students or professors – usually state their theoretical frameworks or biases right away, so that readers can assess the

presentation of the data for themselves. They inform readers of the limitations of their work and tell them about other interpretations that they have rejected.

- **Simplicity:** Academic writing should demonstrate that you have mastered the material and can communicate it effectively *in your own words*. University teachers will challenge you if your words and ideas are expressed in words that are copied and pasted from others. The best way to show that you understand subtle and complex ideas is to put them into simple, but elegant and clear, language.

How to organize an essay

When you start reading a novel, you expect it to use a certain kind of structure. Poems take various forms as well, depending on whether they are sonnets, elegies, or epics. Plays usually have a certain number of acts that vary according to when they were written and the cultural norms in which they were produced. Similarly, academic essays have a basic structure. Once you know the structure, essay writing becomes easier.

The basic structure of an essay consists of a beginning, a middle, and an end. The beginning introduces your subject. The middle develops the various steps in your argument and proves the claims that you made in the introduction. The conclusion sums up what you have argued, proved, and discovered. It may also include any future implications of your findings.

Essay introduction

Getting started is half the battle. Don't make it any harder than it already is. You don't need a dynamic opening to get going. You just need to introduce your topic – the problem, question, or dilemma – followed by any necessary background, and tell the reader what you intend to prove, argue, solve, or review. In other words, the introduction identifies the major problem, controversy, debate, or question to be examined in the essay.

Although this section is brief, it needs to show the value of what is to follow. Depending on the complexity of your topic, the introduction can take up just one paragraph or a couple of pages. There are no absolute rules regarding its length.

In your introduction, it's okay to keep the reader in a bit of suspense. You need to explain your essay topic, but you don't need to state your findings or conclusion. Say, for example, that your paper is on the impact of self-driving cars on the design of cities. In the introduction, you probably don't want to state what the impact will be; instead, state that the topic is an important and interesting one. Try to hook the reader. Once hooked, he or she will want to learn how self-driving cars will affect cities, as argued by you and supported by the evidence that you uncovered during your research.

The introduction ends with a short paragraph that outlines the rest of the essay. Write something like, "The first section of this paper will … The second section will …" Providing an outline at this point means that reading your essay won't feel like being on a roller-coaster ride while wearing a blindfold. Briefly tell the reader what to expect. Using subheadings in the main part of the paper can sometimes be helpful.

Essay body

You can count the number of paragraphs that you need in your essay by adding up two things – your major arguments and the concepts that you need to develop. The usual rule of thumb is that you need at least one paragraph for each concept. These key building blocks are essential in structuring an essay. If you were writing an economics paper, for example, you might discuss the concepts of self-interest, competition, private property, and profits.

If you've done your research well, all of the concepts should already be organized in a computer file, in your mind, or on index cards. It's a good idea to put the concepts on sticky notes or cards so that you can move them around as you begin to compose your essay.

No matter how thoroughly you've organized your research, the process of writing will result in a further reshuffling of your thoughts. Sticky notes allow you to play with concepts without being stuck (if you'll pardon the pun) in one permanent location.

The structure and size of each paragraph depend on how much you need to write to develop each concept. As long as you cover the territory adequately, it doesn't matter whether the paragraphs are long or short. In certain instances, you'll find that you have less to say about some of the concepts. To flesh them out, you may need to do a bit more research.

Concepts are linked together to form arguments. Your primary guide in deciding whether your information and concepts are developed enough is the logical sequence of your argument. As you compose the body of your essay, constantly re-read the paragraphs to ensure that they flow in a logical progression.

You can determine whether your essay flows by asking the following three questions:

1. Can I move backward and forward logically from any point in the essay?
2. Can I quickly diagram my essay on a piece of paper?
3. Can I add greater subtlety or complexity without disrupting the flow?

Essay conclusion

The essay's conclusion must follow logically and clearly from its introduction. You will know that these sections are both strong and complete when you can read just the two of them (omitting the body of the essay) and comprehend the essence of the paper.

One of the tragedies in otherwise intelligent and well-composed essays is a poor conclusion. Many students sabotage their efforts by doing one of the following:

*   Being undecided or wishy-washy ("I'm not sure …").
*   Introducing new ideas or material ("Oh, by the way …").
*   Failing to write a proper conclusion ("Thank goodness it's over!").

The first offence – being uncertain or vague in the conclusion – is hard to avoid by international students. Wanting to play it safe in case the paper might have omitted something crucial, or might not be perfect, or because you don't really trust your arguments or findings, is natural.

International students in particular are often unsure of what is expected in essays and thus are afraid of getting something wrong. Regardless, an indecisive ending is a letdown for the reader who has followed your discussion from start to finish.

Have confidence in your own conclusion. Don't worry about what the professor may think. Any good grader prefers a strong conclusion rather than an essay that just peters out.

The second offence – introducing new ideas or information – is common as well among international students. Usually, students add new information and ideas at the end because they discovered them just as they finished up their essay.

Avoid this situation by not composing your essay at the last minute. That way, if new ideas do occur to you, or you find interesting new facts that are too important to ignore, you still have time to integrate them into the essay itself.

Another way to avoid adding new information in the conclusion is to deal with a tightly focused or narrow topic, question, problem, or dilemma in your essay. Using a general, vague, or broad introduction will, quite naturally, produce more information than can handily be included in your discussion. The result is having to cram in new information at the end of the essay.

In the introduction you can state that you will only examine the impact of autonomous automobiles in developed countries, not developing countries. This avoids having to add material on cities in developing nations in the conclusion.

Regardless of why new information finds its way into the essay, doing so takes your reader's mind off the argument that you've just spent several pages trying to prove. Even worse, it raises questions about what else might be missing from the essay.

TIP 4.1 Avoid using "also" or "in addition" in the concluding section of an essay or report.

The last of these offences – not writing a conclusion at all – is understandable among international students as well. By the time you've developed all your points, you'll probably feel that your job is done. Wrong!

Your essay probably took longer to write than you anticipated. But, you need to write a neat recap of what you've proven or uncovered, or at least underline its significance. There's nothing more irritating than an essay that builds toward a climax but never gets there.

You will know that your conclusion is effective if you feel a sense of closure when you review it. Both you and your reader should feel "been there, done that." Don't leave any loose ends!

Essay writing as a process

Writing an essay is a process, not a mysterious event that occurs on the night before a deadline. The process is explained below.

The first draft

You'll do most of your hard work in creating the first draft of your essay or report. It's where you integrate thinking, research, and writing to craft an argument that:

- establishes a clear thesis, problem, or dilemma;
- addresses and solves a problem;
- demonstrates the effective use of evidence; and
- reflects your own perspective.

Accomplishing all these goals isn't easy, even for experienced writers. At some point in the draft stage, you will almost certainly run into a mental roadblock. When this happens, you can help yourself out by:

- jumping to a different part of the essay, where the writing might flow more easily;
- taking a break, relaxing, and allowing ideas to come without forcing them;
- completing mechanical things such as your title and reference pages;
- writing down what you know and not worrying about what you don't know;

- talking to a teacher or other student about the difficult section; or
- going back and doing more research.

When you're blocked, learning to relax without putting your essay completely out of your mind is the most useful thing you can do. As long as even a small part of your mind remains connected to the paper, your subconscious will work on the problem, and the solution will often just come to you. If you try too hard, your subconscious can't solve the problem for you. Conversely, if you entirely let go of the problem, it may be even bigger when you come back to it.

It's a very good idea to get into the habit of carrying a notebook (paper or electronic), in which you can jot down insights as they occur to you. Experienced professional writers do this. Many even keep a pad and pencil, tablet, or smartphone on the bedside table to jot down any revelations that pop up in the middle of the night. Nothing is more annoying than going back to sleep and finding that your idea has completely evaporated by the next morning!

The second draft

Many great writers have been asked to explain the secret of their success.[2] Their most common answer is: rewriting. Here are tips to rewriting:

- Always wait for a couple of days before you write the second draft; if it's too fresh in your mind, you won't be able to spot any problems objectively.
- Examine what you've written as though it were a classmate's essay rather than your own work.
- Check the transitions between paragraphs. Are they smooth and helpful to the reader?
- Read your essay aloud to determine whether it makes sense and flows well.

Reading your work aloud is an extremely effective communication strategy. Here are a few things you can discover about your paper, simply by reading it aloud:

- Its overall effect, tone, and flow.
- Whether it's focused or unfocused.
- Where the gaps are.
- Which arguments work and which don't.
- Whether it repeats itself.

This strategy can be even more effective if you tape yourself reading and then listen to the playback.

It's not a good idea to focus on spelling or the rules of grammar during this stage. Once you begin a word-by-word edit, you simply can't engage in creative problem-solving at the same time. You also lose the ability to see your essay from the point of view of an interested reader.

The final draft

The final draft is the right place to do the fine editing that every paper needs. Now is the time to go over grammar, punctuation, spelling, and word choice. Many international students write strong papers with plenty of research, but then struggle with language problems.

Spell checking software certainly make the final editing process a lot easier than formerly and are especially helpful for international students. Make sure to use all the spelling and grammar features available. But it is still up to you to perform the close and careful check that can make the difference between earning a B or an A on your assignment.

Students often wonder why they are penalized for mistakes that have nothing to do with thinking. Here are four reasons:

1. Spelling errors and typos are signs of sloppiness, rushing, and lack of attention. Errors on the cover page or introduction are particularly detrimental. In the "real world," such as when applying for jobs, spelling errors and typos are not tolerated.
2. A limited vocabulary prevents you from communicating what you really mean.

3. Poor punctuation detracts from the flow of your essay, forcing the reader to go over the sentence more than once to decipher it.
4. Weak grammar reduces the force of a sentence or paragraph and often changes or garbles its meaning.

Editing

It is very difficult, and often impossible, to edit your own prose. It's hard to find the problems, both grammatical and substantive, in your writing. No author can possibly edit his or her own work expertly. This is even more so for international students writing in a new language.

With editing you need to enlist the help of others. These can be classmates, friends, people "back home," or others. Parents can help as well, but may be too supportive, responding with "Darling, this is the best thing you've ever written." Such sentiments are not helpful.

Find colleagues who are critical, who will question you, and who will point out flaws, problems, inconsistencies, and any other form of weakness. When you find such people, treat them very well. Their input will considerably improve your essay's grade.

Incidentally, the best way to keep good editors is to reciprocate. They will give your papers as much attention as you give theirs. If you are not as good an editor as they are, reciprocate in other ways.

Your university likely have services to help with writing and editing. Be sure to take advantage of these especially early in the school term when the services are not overwhelmed. As an international student you may have more specialized services available to support your academic performance. Take advantage of these, but realize that they will teach you the skills, but not do the writing or editing for you.

Citing sources and plagiarism

Many essay writers have problems with citing material from books, articles, and the internet. International students have even more problems in this regard. Let's make sure you don't encounter any.

The general rule is that you must reference both ideas and facts that you acquired from reading books, articles, websites, and others sources, whether you include them in the form of a direct quote or rephrase them in your own words. If you are copying material (that is, copying and pasting), you must put it in quotation marks to show that the words are not your own and to reveal your source.

But what can get confusing is that "common knowledge" does not require you to include a source. For example, an assignment that includes a sentence on the theory of gravity, will not generally require a mention of Isaac Newton and his writings. That is because it is common knowledge that Newton was the first to write a scientific account of gravity. On the other hand, if you are writing about recent developments in quantum gravity then you will be expected to cite articles or books on what is quantum gravity and who first used this term.

Often students decide that someone else – like an expert – summarized or expressed something much better than they possibly could. This is even more so with international students who may be writing in a language that is new to them. Why not just use the wonderful description or explanation found in the book, article, or website? You can do so, but only if you clearly reference it and place the words, phrases, or sentence you copied in quotation marks. Doing so avoids plagiarism and you need not worry.

But what about if you take the original work and passage and rewrite it in your own words. That's still plagiarism! You still need to make reference in your assignment of the original passage. This way you demonstrate that you used it to craft your own words.

What often causes headaches, and much worse, for international students is that what is called plagiarism by teachers and professors varies from place to place. In some countries is may be generally acceptable to copy and paste a phrase or even a sentence without attribution. In other countries, this is not.

Our advice is to write assignments as much as possible using your own words, not those of others. The prose may not be as clear and beautiful, but your professor or grader will know it is you writing, not someone else. If you believe that you are using ideas, phrases or material that come from others, be sure to reference it. More referencing or citations is much better than less.

In any case, be prepared that plagiarism is an area in which international students can find themselves in unexpected trouble.

> **TIP 4.2**   Look at this website to help you better understand what is plagiarism: www.plagiarism.org/article/what-is-plagiarism

You can also use technology to help you. There are some free online plagiarism checkers. You might use these to check one of your assignments so see what the result is. There are more advanced versions that require you to pay a modest cost. Again, you might try these for a few assignments to determine what they reveal about your writing.

But first check your university's websites (the library, writing centre, or international student centre). You might find a free plagiarism checker there! You will certainly find advice and help to understand what plagiarism is and how to avoid it.

You will not be an expert in shunning plagiarism right away. But this is a topic that ought to be near the top of your to-do list to ensure success in your international studies.

Citation styles

Citation or referencing is how you show to the reader what sources you are employing in writing a particular sentence or paragraph. There are different ways to do so.

If you are directed to use a particular citation style, either that developed by the American Psychological Association (APA) or the Modern Language Association (MLA), be sure to apply it throughout. You can find more information online about how to use these.

If you're at liberty to choose a style, use just one and be consistent. If you're unsure, simply adopt whatever style is used in your textbook or other key books in the course.

Perhaps the easiest way of citing a source is by using the author–date style. This is a simple and easy to use style. The examples below give three different ways of using an author–date citation in a sentence:

Example 1: One observer writes that "in the second decade of the twenty-first century, inequalities of wealth that had supposedly disappeared are close to regaining or even surpassing their historical highs" (Piketty, 2014, p. 471).

Example 2: Thomas Piketty (2014) writes that at the present time "inequalities of wealth that had supposedly disappeared are close to regaining or even surpassing their historical highs" (p. 471).

Example 3: One view of the new global economy is that inequality is rising to levels not seen for decades (Piketty, 2014, p. 471).

Note that in Example 3 you still needed to cite Thomas Piketty's book even though the sentence is one that you wrote. That is, the sentence is not found on page 471 of the book. However, the main idea in the sentence is from Piketty's book, which is why must tell the reader, using a citation, where you got it from.

Your list of references at the end of your essay or report will include the following entry:

REFERENCES

Piketty, Thomas. 2014. *Capital in the Twenty-First Century*, translated by Arthur Goldhammer. Cambridge, MA: Harvard University Press.

If you found a source on the internet, add the URL link at the end of the entry, and give the date that you read it, such as "accessed on 14 November 2018."

If you are stuck, look to the internet for guides on how to cite sources correctly in your school assignments. Your university and perhaps your course will also have resources to help you.

Title page

When you perform your final edit, don't forget the title of your paper. Regardless of its length or content, every assignment, essay, and report should have a unique, meaningful, and engaging title.

Do you like watching movies and films? Look at the amount of time and creativity that goes into the title sequence. There's a reason for that. The title sequence tells you what to expect and makes sure you're in the right frame of mind.

The same applies to written assignments. The title should not simply reword the assignment question but should give the reader some insight into what the paper contains. Would you be impressed by a film title like *Movie #1*? A thoughtful and intriguing title puts the reader in the right disposition when starting to read.

The title page also includes basic information such as the date, course number, department or school name, your name and student number, and the name of the professor, teaching assistant, or marker. Make it interesting (perhaps with a graphic or image) since it sets the tone for the rest. If you sense that your professor seems a stickler for rules, ask if he or she has any specific preferences, since sometimes professors do not like diagrams, graphics, or unusual fonts in an assignment.

At this stage, you may also want to add an interesting quotation on the first page of the essay. Many authors of novels, short stories, and even poets, do so as a good way of gaining the attention and interest of readers.

You may have noticed that every chapter in this book is headed with a quote. All of them were chosen carefully for meaning and relevance. The quotation at the start of this chapter highlights that many small steps are the basis of our accomplishments. Last but not least, also ensure that you have numbered the pages in your paper.

Common essay-writing errors

If you need extra work in English grammar, seek help from your university's writing centre, international student office, or a private tutor. There are also online services that will be of value. Professors and teaching assistants will not be much use in improving language skills as they don't have the time required.

Don't hesitate to seek help, as you'll swiftly improve your writing skills and your grades! Grammar is learned quickly, so the necessary investment in time (and money) will be small, but will remain with you for the rest of your life.

English is a confounding language with exceptions to every rule and then exceptions to the exceptions.[3] Here are some grammatical and essay-writing mistakes that you can easily fix on your own.

Overuse of the passive voice

The following sentence contains two examples of the passive voice: "The meeting was called to order, and the budget was presented." Rewritten to use the active voice, the sentence reads, "The president called the meeting to order, and the treasurer presented the budget."

Sometimes it's difficult to avoid the passive voice. Using it too much, however, significantly reduces the clarity and force of your thoughts. Students often employ passive constructions to evade identifying the subject of a sentence. For example, a student might write, "This was seen to be an important problem." A good marker will ask, "By whom?"

Vague pronouns

Avoid using pronouns, such as "it" in a vague manner. For instance, saying "It was good last night" leaves the reader in the dark about what might have been good.

Tense confusion

A common, and distracting, grammatical error is the incorrect use of tenses. This forces readers to go back over the sentence to ensure that they've understood it. If your essay begins with the past tense, it needs to continue in this tense (unless there's a logical reason to change it). In any case, always be aware of what tense you're using.

Possessive use

Many people, including native English speakers, have difficulty with the possessive form, like the robins' nest or the cat's tail. There is also confusion between "its" versus "it's."

"Its" is the possessive form – "The company failed to meet its profit targets." "The cat chased its tail."

"It's" is a shortened version of "it is" or "it has." You can write any sentence in English without having to add an "s" for the possessive. "The robins' nest" is simply "the nest of the robins" and "the cat's tail" is "the tail of the cat."

If you are unsure about possessives you can generally find a way to reword a sentence to avoid the possessive form. Rather than writing, "My friend's house is beyond the hill," just write "The house of my friend is beyond the hill."

Common spelling errors

Some spelling mistakes are made much more often than others. Remember the following:

- *Compliment* means to say something nice: "He paid me a compliment about my report."
- *Complement* means to fit together: "Her work complements my work."
- *Principle* (noun) refers to a rule: "A principle of the legal system is the right to a lawyer."
- *Principal* (adjective) means most important: "The principal character in the play is the mother."
- *Principal* (noun) is a person in a position of leadership: "A principal heads the school."
- *Affect* (usually a verb) means to influence: "My gender affected my chances."
- *Effect* (usually a noun) is a result or consequence: "The effect of the treatment was successful."
- *Effect* (sometimes a verb) means to bring about: "I will effect a change in my life."

Lab reports and similar assignments

Although the above sections deal primarily with essays, many of the comments apply to other types of writing that you may do in university, whether they be book reviews, journals, or blogs.

A lab report is something of an exception, however. It is fairly restrictive and formulaic, so be sure that you know exactly what is required and don't deviate from it.

Case studies are more concise and business-like in style and have an organization all of their own. They move rapidly from description and analysis to an optimal solution. However, they do leave room to explore alternatives and to demonstrate critical and even creative thinking.

The last word

This chapter has provided specific tools and suggestions for bettering your performance on exams and written assignments as an international student. You can also use them to improve many areas of your schoolwork that need attention. However, remember that you need time and determination to obtain the results you desire.[4]

Just as Disneyland wasn't built overnight, becoming a good writer takes time, especially if not in your native language. But in the classroom, and then later in the workplace, there are few skills that have a bigger payoff than the ability to express complex thoughts, ideas, or facts in clear written form.

Notes

1   For a perspective from a professor on literature and literary basics, see Thomas C. Foster, *How to Read Literature Like a Professor: A Lively and Entertaining Guide to Reading Between the Lines* (New York: Harper, 2014).

2   Stephen King's books have sold more than 350 million copies, making him the world's bestselling novelist. His advice for writers is in *On Writing: A Memoir of the Craft* (New York: Scribners, 2010).

3   To see how English developed from a language originally spoken only by peasants see Bill Bryson, *The Mother Tongue: English and How It Got That Way* (London: Penguin, 2009).

4   If you're looking for more assistance with writing assignments in your courses, look at Stephen Bailey, *Academic Writing: A Handbook for International Students* (New York: Routledge, 2011).

Essential classroom skills (II)

Oral presentations, group work, and becoming a proactive learner

> *If something comes from your heart, it will reach the heart of your audience.*
>
> Fawzia Koofi

Introduction

Among the most disliked classroom experiences by international students are oral presentations and group work. But if you can master these and related activities, your study abroad experience will be more satisfying and less nerve-wracking. Lastly, feeling more comfortable giving presentations and in performing group work will also help in your post-graduation employment.

Effective presentations and teamwork will earn you high grades, and are excellent ways for international students to make more friends. To improve your performance in both these areas, and others, you will need to be a proactive student. Becoming more proactive means learning how to take first-rate notes, being organized, and dealing effective with distractions. Let this chapter show you how.

Let's begin with oral presentations.

Oral presentations

For many international students, giving a presentation in a class is one of the worst parts of their learning. Being in front of an audience is not fun at the best of times, and even less so in a place that is unfamiliar with people you may not know.

Overall, presentations are stressful, preparing them is time consuming, and you never quite know what to expect. Yet, if you master them, your future is bright.

There are many types of oral presentations. At the formal end of the continuum, you may have to stand in front of a class and speak on a topic of your instructor's or your own choosing. But there are many more types of oral presentations: asking or answering a question during class or in the professor's office, introducing yourself in class or outside, seeking information from a librarian, and many more. Some international study applicants are interviewed as part of the application process either in person or electronically.

After you graduate, there will be many more oral presentations. Without good presentation skills, you will have great difficulty even landing a job. After all, the first oral presentation for your employer will be your employment interview!

Presentations will play a major role in your life after graduation. Regardless of your job, you'll give many presentations. You will be responsible for explaining something, communicating your ideas to others, and encouraging the people with whom you interact. Your audiences will include customers, clients, investors, colleagues, supervisors, and perhaps the general public. Even if you don't give many presentations in your first job, you'll probably prepare them for your supervisor.

Why oral presentations?

You may think that oral presentations are overrated, but consider why professors (and many others like employers) choose them rather than other modes of conveying information or ideas:

- Presentations are the most personalized delivery of material. Think of how powerful they are at persuading an audience to buy a product or accept an idea. As well, presentations are all you! Alone on stage.
- Half of all interpersonal communication takes the form of facial expressions and body language.

- The printed page cannot easily display the rhetorical styles and devices that are available to a good speaker. He or she can pause for effect, adjust to feedback, change tone and emphasis, point, and invite and answer questions.
- A well-prepared and well-delivered presentation demonstrates a real commitment to the audience. By showing this level of respect for their listeners, speakers earn far greater respect for their subject matter than is possible in any other format.

With the importance of social media, presentation skills are more sought after than ever. Would you rather watch a talk or lecture on YouTube or read a text-only version? Would you rather buy a product that is being demonstrated and described by an individual, rather than only reading a brochure about the product? Would you rather watch a political debate, or read the transcript?

> **TIP 5.1** Nothing is more effective or compelling than enthusiasm. The best presenters are those who convey personal passion. Your language skills might be limited and your knowledge of the material as well, but enthusiasm alone will give you a pretty awesome presentation.

Key skills for presentations

Do you think some people are just better at verbal communication than others? The truth is that anyone can significantly improve this skill. Treat presentations as an opportunity to develop a useful skill, to demonstrate your ability to simplify material, and to really impress your instructors and classmates (and more importantly, yourself).

When you are good at something difficult, it becomes satisfying and even pleasurable. Giving presentations is obviously difficult, so delivering an effective one can be amazing. Just check out the faces of your classmates following a successful presentation.

Here are some easy-to-use tips for presentations that you can adapt to your own situation.

Preparing for the big day

- If a course requires a formal presentation, try to schedule it early in the term, when there are fewer conflicts with tests and other assignments. But avoid being the first or second presentation, so you can see how other students perform.
- Presentations are so much easier if the topic interests you. After all, why speak on something that bores you? Even if you're stuck with a bad presentation topic – perhaps because others snagged all the good ones, or the professor assigned it to you – don't settle for mediocrity.
- Be proactive. Always think of a presentation as a chance to impress everyone, not just with how hard you've worked, but also with how clever and original you've been.
- Stage a dress rehearsal. Practice makes perfect. Practise in front of a mirror, friends or camera.
- Watch for mannerisms. Everyone has nervous tics. Identify, eliminate, or transform them into useful gestures by practising in a mirror or taping yourself.

The day of the presentation

- Appearance matters. Dress well to show everyone how serious you are about your talk and how much you respect your audience.
- Arrive early. Check all your equipment. Go over your notes. Decide how you intend to start the presentation.

Starting the presentation

- Don't start with "Uhm, I guess it's my turn." Rather start with "It is wonderful to be here!"
- Provide a warm welcome. Get your audience on your side right away. Introduce both yourself and your topic. Remember that your listeners want you to succeed.
- Appear confident and composed, even if your stomach is full of butterflies.

During the presentation

- Talk directly to your audience. Never read from notes if you can help it, and don't over-prepare so as to become mechanical. Refer to your notes only if you get stuck.
- Vary the activities. Remember that listeners have a short attention span.
- Present the audience with a clear summary that can be useful as a study guide for an exam. Your fellow students will enjoy your presentation that much more if it also saves them some work.
- Always try to have at least one surprise up your sleeve. If you can provide extra value that no one expected, your presentation will be memorable. If appropriate, bring candy or other goodies to distribute, or a small souvenir from your home country. Be creative in this.

Ending the presentation

- Finish on a strong note and don't be overly modest. False modesty is for losers. Winners try to leave with a bang. Don't say "Uh, I guess I'm finished now." Rather end with "Thank you very much. You've been a great audience!"
- No one enjoys criticism, but try to see it as constructive. Don't be defensive if questions are asked after your talk. Respond briefly and positively, with something like, "You make a really good point, thank you."

Especially for international students

International students are especially prone to five problems in making presentations. These are listed below, with ways to minimize them.

Not projecting clearly

The greatest presentation in the world is useless if no one can hear it. Many presenters speak too quietly. This is particularly the case when speaking in a language that is not native, or in a situation that is uncomfortable. People who give an inaudible talk send this message to the audience: I don't want to be here, and I don't know my material.

Talk louder than you think is necessary or than you are comfortable doing. Talk slower than you usually do.

Not making eye contact

One advantage of a presentation is the interaction and rapport with the audience. This requires making eye contact with listeners. The failure to do so is a sign of uncertainty and lack of engagement with the audience. Often international students are unsure of the rules about eye contact in their new environment. For presentations in university environments regardless of place, eye contact with the audience is essential.

Look at the audience as much as possible. Select two or three friendly faces and speak to them.

Giving too much information

As an international student you are under pressure to perform well. One way to do that is just to load up facts, figures, diagrams, slides, and more for your presentation. Identify what absolutely must be conveyed and omit the rest. No presentation will communicate all, or even most, of what you know. Just hit the highlights.

Running over time

How do you feel about instructors who keep talking after the class has ended? There is no better way to sabotage an otherwise good presentation than by going over time. Doing so tells your listeners that your time is more important than theirs, which completely defeats the atmosphere of mutual respect that you've been trying to create.

If you suspect that you won't finish on time, simply leave things out. The audience won't notice. To avoid running over time, give a talk that's shorter than its allotted period. This ensures that you will finish on time.

Using audio-visual aids inappropriately

Don't be seduced by technology! For international students being able to show slides is a life saver, but a successful presentation depends on more than whiz-bang audio-visual effects. If you project slides on a screen, don't just read them. Rather use them to guide and highlight your main themes.

> **TIP 5.2** If you are using PowerPoint or other projected materials, the rule of thumb is one slide per minute at the most. Yes, one slide!

Replying to questions

For many international students, the most stressful part of a presentation is when the audience asks questions, especially the professor. Set the ground rules right away to favour your strengths. If you'd prefer not to answer questions until the end, say so at the beginning. On the other hand, if you want to maintain an interactive atmosphere, you can ask the audience to raise questions as your talk unfolds.

Encouraging listeners to ask questions is a good way of inviting them into a relationship with you. It's your invitation, rather than the questions themselves, that is most important in bonding with the audience.

Make your invitation genuine. Don't just say "Any questions?" very quietly and then immediately sit down and pray no one asks any. Give the audience a chance to interact with you. Say something along the lines of "I'd love to hear some questions" or "Is there anything that you'd like me to clarify or explore further?"

Maintain eye contact with the audience. Smile. Wait. Twenty seconds can seem like twenty minutes when you're waiting for someone to speak up, but people need time to shift from listening mode to questioning mode. Wait for this to happen.

Whenever you get a question, repeat it for the audience. This will demonstrate that you see it as important (and will gratify the questioner) and will also invite everyone in the room to share in it. Doing this will ensure that you understood the question, which is especially important for international students.

Never bluff or lose your composure. You're not expected to know everything. If you don't know the answer, say so: "That's a *really* good question! I don't know the answer but I will be happy to get the information by our next class."

When someone asks a weak or off-topic question, convert it into a good one, using it as an opportunity to demonstrate your skill and really win over your audience. Seasoned presenters are adept at finding a grain of brilliance in a bad question and turning it to their advantage. The inquirer will rarely challenge the interpretation, since the question has been reworked into something that puts him or her in a flattering light. The perceptive people in the audience will appreciate that an awkward situation has been handled without slighting the individual's dignity. It's a win–win situation for everyone.

Most imperative, **never, ever** get defensive and try to justify yourself in response to questions. It's hard to hear "You've left this out!" or "I don't agree!" or even "You're wrong!" from audience members. These kinds of comments may make you feel bad, especially if as an international student you spent much time and energy to prepare your presentation.

The instinctive reaction to feeling attacked is to launch into a lengthy explanation or repeat parts of your talk. Don't put yourself in this position. Instead, answer briefly and don't hesitate to say "That's an excellent point you've made and something I will consider."

Always thank your listeners for asking questions, and tell them that they've been a good audience. If you make this point, they're bound to conclude that you're an effective presenter!

Hopefully, you now begin to see oral presentations not so much as chores, but as something valuable, interesting, and even fun. We now discuss another activity that international students often dislike but that is vital for success in school and then in the workplace.

Group work

Many students see group projects as a waste of precious time, and does not recognize their individual effort. This is because not everyone contributes equally. International students often struggle in groups as they may not completely understand what is required, or how to best interact with team members.

Sometimes international students are the last ones to be assigned to teams as native students may want to avoid having them as group members, fearing they don't speak the local language well or will not contribute adequately.

Lastly, group work is the most unpredictable type of school assignment. You don't know how it will turn out and you have little control of the final grade. But group work is essential in school and then later. In the world of work, people rarely operate in isolation. The success of companies and organizations is based on effective collaboration.

Today's business community and employer marketplace are big on collaboration. Given this, it's not surprising that all presentations in business schools and many other professional university programmes are given by teams.

Despite these obvious advantages and benefits, teamwork has its drawbacks. Almost always there are differences among team members about how to proceed; disagreements that take time to resolve; and not everyone works equally hard.

However, you must learn to deal with these frustrations to complete your international studies. Furthermore, in your future job, you will work primarily in groups. Most activities are group-based. In fact, functioning well in a team setting will get you jobs, whereas the inability to do this will cost you jobs and promotions.

Improving teamwork

Here are six easy-to-use tips that can be adapted to any team or group situation:

1. Always engage in a group brainstorming session before deciding on a strategy. Don't let one person dictate the plan. Everyone needs to have ownership of the assignment or project.
2. Ensure that everyone has a specific role to play in the project. But also make sure that everyone understands that this

does not absolve him or her of responsibility for the project as a whole.

3. Decide what to do if someone is not contributing to the team. Have this discussion during the first group meeting.

4. Ask your instructor for help in dealing with people who don't pull their weight. But before approaching your professor be sure to marshal the evidence required to show that the team member is not participating and what has been tried. Professors want facts before taking action.

5. If there is an oral presentation then act as a team during the presentation or project. If you have no role to play at a particular time, your job is to support what your colleagues are doing. Keep eye contact with the team member presenting at a given time.

6. Achieve closure. Celebrate the project's completion with your colleagues. However briefly, you were an effective team and you want to show each other gratitude and respect.

The real magic of group work is that what you can achieve in partnership with others is a quantum leap over what you can achieve alone. The destination is well worth any frustration encountered along the way, and the time spent is well spent.

Being a proactive international student

Being successful in oral presentations and group work entails being a proactive individual. As an international student you most likely already are. But you may have to stretch yourself to fully succeed in your studies and thereafter.

Proactive individuals, sometimes referred to as self-starters, are in high demand by employers at public and private organizations. Unlike reactive individuals, proactive people work and plan ahead rather than reacting to problems or situations. At school as an international student, demonstrate the professionalism that you intend to exhibit in the workforce.

Submit your assignments on time, and don't be late for, or skip, class. Read the syllabus carefully. Do your reading before class so that you can benefit from the instructor's interpretation. If you treat your classes casually, chances are that you'll treat your future job in just the same way.

Moreover, as an international student you may have to catch up on the local language and knowledge. It makes sense to score the easy grades by being on time and organized, and generally pro-active. In other words, why make your courses more difficult than need be the case?

Let's take a minute to think about grades. The real reason why potential employers and graduate programmes are interested in your grades is because students who earn good grades are con-scientious, dedicated, and proactive about the specific tasks. An "A" grade implies being well prepared and going beyond what is expected.

Try to figure things out on your own, in a creative manner, rather than running to your teaching assistant or professor with every question. You'll be surprised how much you can solve on your own with research, technology, and ingenuity.

There will be times when you need something from a professor, librarian, or teaching assistant. Again, approach this situation like a professional – prepare your evidence or question, rehearse, and try to analyse the situation. Remember the rules for oral presentations.

> **TIP 5.3** Don't ask professors how to get better grades. Rather ask your professor how you might better understand material or improve your performance. When you better understand the material and expectations, your grades will improve.

Asking for a deadline extension on the day that an assignment is due may be acceptable in some courses but this approach will cer-tainly limit your studies and future opportunities. Having a break-down in front of your professor because of stress, lack of sleep, or poor diet the day before the final exam may win you sympathy as a first year undergraduate student, and as an international student. A similar collapse in front of your boss or client will cost you a pro-motion, if not your job.

You may believe that university and work are so different that you can be late with school assignments, write your papers the night before the deadline, cram for exams, miss classes, do the minimum, and be disorganized, but that as soon as you graduate you will become a different person.

In a few rare cases this may true, but the way you handle your time as an international student is a good predictor of what you'll be like after graduation. Certainly, potential employers have this view based on many years of hiring university graduates.

An important fact to consider is that some of your classmates, and even professors, may ultimately become your clients, colleagues, or customers. Entrepreneurs and senior executives often appoint their university friends to top positions.

Managers who are looking for new employees often consult with their acquaintances for contacts. Informal networking and word of mouth are sometimes as important as formal job applications. See Chapter 6 to learn more about networking and its crucial role in the labour market. Always demonstrate to those around you that you are a proactive person rather than reactive one.

In being proactive, don't forget the learning that occurs outside of classrooms. There likely are dozens if not hundreds of clubs, sports teams, associations, and theatre groups and many other organizations at your university that allow you to learn, meet new people and have fun.

Many organizations, when they hire recent graduates check résumés for evidence of involvement in school clubs, athletics, and other extra-curricular activities. Why? Because employers are impressed by someone who can combine academics with extra-curricular activities; it demonstrates balance, commitment, a willingness to work hard, and teamwork.

Taking notes

Note taking may strike you as not very relevant, and perhaps even arcane now with the possibility of creating audio and digital files. You may think that taking notes in class, and from textbooks, is unique to university and you'll never be doing that again. In fact, quite the opposite!

Taking good notes is integral to succeeding as an international student and essential to just about any professional occupation that you can name. Note taking is a defining characteristic of a proactive and high-performing person.

For example, healthcare professionals, journalists, bankers and financial advisers, social workers, police officers, teachers, and lawyers must take very detailed notes concerning clients and events. Their notes may become critical pieces of evidence in courts of law, often years after they were written.

Teachers keep notes on the progress of students, which are summarized later in the form of report cards, grades, letters of reference, and other documents. Journalists and other writers depend on their skills in taking notes. Financial advisers make notes of the preferences and investment advice of their clients and must be able to recall this information quickly.

At any important meeting in the public or private sector, someone will take notes. For your first few years in the workforce, you may be required to prepare the minutes of various meetings.

You can be assured that many times during your career, you will be asked to "Attend tomorrow's meeting for me and take notes so that I'll know what happened" or to "Read over this report and write me a summary." Doing this well will get you noticed and rewarded. Doing it poorly will only get you noticed.

The keys to creating good notes in university are the same as those in the professional world after graduation: clarity, conciseness, and precision. But writing notes at school is easier because no one else will read them other than you, whereas in the workforce other people will often use your notes.

When taking notes at a lecture or class aim to:

- summarize complex information succinctly;
- organize material in a meaningful way (the lecture may have been unfocused, but your notes should be the opposite);
- highlight the key ideas and clarify their significance;
- include the insights from various sources (the speaker, readings, questions asked, past events); and
- pinpoint areas and problems that require further exploration.

Telltale signs of ineffective note taking by international students are:

- furiously trying to record everything (remember: notes are a summary); and
- notes that are either disjointed or poorly organized.

Techniques that can develop your skill as a note taker in university:

- always reading the materials that relate to the lecture beforehand;
- leaving spaces in your notes to add new ideas later;
- creating your own shorthand to remind you of important connections or questions (such as =,?, >>);
- re-reading your notes while they are still fresh and making any connections or embellishments that you could not develop during the lecture;
- answering any questions that you posed in your notes, either by consulting the readings, other students, or your teacher;
- regularly summarizing all your notes on a particular course unit or section; and
- comparing your notes with those of other students in your class or study group.

We can tell you with some authority that the ability to take good notes makes a major difference between international students who do well in their coursework and those who struggle.

Many students use a computer to take notes, and some classes even require them to do this. Our recommendation is to use pen and paper. This is because taking notes with a computer or tablet is a temptation to multi-task – to search for information online, play games, watch movies, or even visit social networks.

Multi-tasking during lectures, no matter how appealing, reduces grades. Don't believe us? Check the studies that compared students who handwrote their notes to those who used laptops.[1] Taking good notes, and earning good grades, is best done sitting in the middle or near the front of a classroom, with your smartphone and computer turned off. Choosing a seat in the back row is not conducive to learning, and a smartphone distracts from an activity that requires your full attention.[2] Make a habit of sitting close to the front, and you will quickly find that listening and taking notes is easier and more fulfilling.

■ Getting yourself organized

It can be hard to get organized. Sometimes we're not motivated by the task we need to complete (like studying for a test in a course that is boring), or we're distracted, which is all too easy for international students who are in a new and highly stimulating environment.

Students often do things at the last minute, not because they're lazy, but because it's a quick method of organizing and motivating themselves. The eighteenth-century writer and inventor of the modern dictionary for the English language, Samuel Johnson, once remarked that a person could really get focused on the night before his execution.[3] Some students seem to share this view, and some will even claim that they do their best work on the night before the deadline.

Teachers and experienced students know that this is not true, as do successful professionals. Would you like to be operated on by an overly stressed and exhausted surgeon who does their work while drinking high-caffeine beverages? Do you want to be represented by a lawyer who didn't sleep on the night before your court date and cannot focus?

Time is the most precious commodity that an international university student has; that's why using it well is so important.[4]

Below are five suggestions to assist you in managing your time:

1. Make yourself follow a routine. This is especially important for an international student in a new environment. Try to get up at the same time each morning and go to bed at the same time each night during school days.
2. Create a schedule for your academic term that includes all due dates for assignments and exams.
3. Most courses, to the frustration of students, are back-end-loaded. In other words, the bulk of the work is required late in the term. Minimize this "crunch time" by planning and working far in advance of deadlines.
4. Identify priorities. Some subjects or assignments are more important than others. Spending a lot of time on an unimportant task is a waste of time.

5.   Aim for steady improvement rather than perfection. This advice is especially important for students who face a period of adjustment. You're bound to be lousy at things when you first do them. That's life. What's important is getting better over time.

Deal effectively with distractions

The French existentialist philosopher Jean-Paul Sartre once wrote that "Hell is other people."[5] Distractions can be a particular problem for international students. After all, you're in a new environment with lots of exciting sights and people; perhaps an entire continent to explore before you head home in a few weeks or months.

If you are living in a dormitory, you will have lots of new friends, and your friends and family from back home may come to visit you. School assignments and responsibilities sure can get in the way!

Most people don't understand, don't remember, or conveniently forget the intrusiveness of interruptions and can be offended if you tell them, "Sorry, but I'm working on a project. I'll call you later."

How you deal with these disruptions can shape your student experience and even your career. The students who deal firmly but gently with such distractions usually achieve the greatest success, and have the most fun.

Here are seven tips on reducing distractions while also making new friends, and keeping your existing friends:

1.   Let people know when you are busy and not able to see them, and when you will be available.
2.   Be firm, so that they'll understand that your school work is important to you.
3.   Be consistent, so that they'll know where they stand and will realize that you're not rejecting them.
4.   Follow up with them when you're free to do so.

5.   Give them your full attention when you connect with them. That way, they will come to value the quality rather than the quantity of time that they spend with you.
6.   Make friends with people whose goals and objectives resemble yours, and who appreciate the importance of focused attention.
7.   Combine social interaction with academic achievement by forming a study group. Some terrific friendships and future networks get their start in study groups.

One reason for being an international student is to meet people and make new friends. The friendships you make at your school can, and often do, last a lifetime. It's only when you let your social life interfere too much with your academic life that a problem emerges.

On the other hand, over-privileging their social life is the main reason why international students struggle and fail. The temptation can seem overwhelming, especially when you are released from the constraints of your usual environment. But, if you take a proactive approach and use the strategies of this chapter, your international study experience will be full of learning and fun.

Notes

1   See Pam A. Mueller and Daniel M. Oppenheimer, "The Pen is Mightier than the Keyboard: Advantages of Longhand over Laptop Note Taking," *Psychological Science* 25(6) (2014): 1159–1168.
2   Faria Sana, Tina Weston and Nicholas J. Cepeda, "Laptop Multitasking Hinders Classroom Learning for both users and Nearby Peers," *Computers and Education* 62 (2013): 24–31.
3   Samuel Johnson (1709–1784). For a biography of this interesting and in many ways modern man, see Peter Martin, *Samuel Johnson: A Biography* (Cambridge, MA: Harvard University Press, 2008).
4   Some examples of interesting books about time are: Ron Fry, *Manage Your Time* (London: Kogan Page, 1997), Peter Levin,

Skilful Time Management (Maidenhead: Open University Press, 2007) and Lyn Underwood, *Study Time Management* (Cippenham: Foulsham, 1996).

5   Jean-Paul Sartre (1905–1980) was a French philosopher and writer. He was awarded the 1964 Nobel Prize for Literature. For more information see Anthony Hatzimoysis, *The Philosophy of Sartre* (New York: Routledge, 2013).

The Triple M career roadmap
Me, market, and match

CHAPTER 6

Me and market
Knowing yourself and potential employers

It is wisdom to know others; it is enlightenment to know one's self.

Lao-Tzu

Introduction

After much hard work – and hopefully as much fun – your time as a student is coming to an end. Quite rightly your priorities shift to preparing for your first full-time post-degree job.

As an international student, you might be thinking not only about studying abroad but also working in a country other than your own. Or you might be returning home after some months or years abroad.

Looking for, and then obtaining, your dream job will not be easy. You know the competition is fierce and opportunities are limited. The world of work is changing dramatically. Due to automation-enabled technology such as robotics and artificial intelligence many jobs will disappear, while others will grow and new ones, which we haven't heard of yet, will be created. This means that it is very important that you prepare yourself for the future by being self-aware and willing to adapt to a constantly changing environment.

The recent World Economic Future of Jobs report[1] suggests that over one-third of skills that are considered important today will change within the next five years. It also suggests that while proficiency in new technology will become more important so will "human skills" such as creativity and emotional intelligence. As an international learner you might have developed these skills already. It is important that you are able to identify your skills and are willing to develop these and other skills further to stay relevant in your future career.

This chapter, and the next two, show you that although the road from school to a great career is not one you have travelled before, it can be a smooth one. Utilizing lots of examples we show you how to prepare yourself for the transition.

The first part of the chapter will help you more fully understand what you wish for in your career; while the second part of the chapter shows you what employment opportunities are available for you.

The Triple M Career Roadmap

We've created the Triple M Career Roadmap to provide you with a guide on how to start your career abroad, or back home. As illustrated in Figure 6.1, the map has three steps in the transition from school to full-time work. Let's look at each in turn.

- **Step 1 – Me:** Knowing yourself is the first step in finding your dream job. You need to identify your career vision and your values, interests, personality, and skills (VIPS) using self-assessments and personality profiles. Some of this can be done by visiting the career office at your university. Experienced career advisers will help you to analyse and identify what career might suit you. However, as we teach you in the first part of this chapter, you can also start to explore your VIPS on your own.

STEP 1: "Me"	STEP 2: "Market"	STEP 3: "Match"
Know Yourself	Know the Market	Match Yourself and the Market

Figure 6.1 Triple M Career Roadmap

- **Step 2 – Market:** Knowing the market entails learning about the employers in the location you wish to find work. You will need to conduct research on their culture and hiring practices, and on the nature of the employment positions that are available to individuals like you. Visit career events organized by your career office at university, attend job fairs, go to company visits and the recruiting activities of employers, find a mentor, and speak with alumni – all of this will help you make more informed decisions about potential career paths. More importantly, however, is conducting informational interviews and networking, both of which we teach you in the second part of this chapter.
- **Step 3 – Match:** You need to match yourself with the market. Once you know what jobs you are looking for you can apply for specific positions that align with your VIPS. When looking for an employment position you will need a résumé and be prepared for interviews. In Chapter 7 we show you how you write a résumé and cover letter that will wow potential employers, and in Chapter 8 you will learn how to ace the interview.

Step 1: Me

The first step in the Triple M Career Roadmap is the most important, as it lays the foundation for the next steps in your career journey. The earlier you begin with Step 1 the better. You should not start assessing your VIPS (values, interests, personality, and skills) once you are about to graduate but already while studying.

Doing so will help you immensely later in job searching when you will have to draft your application package, including your résumé and cover letter, and convince employers to hire you in an interview. Once you have identified your VIPS you can easily identify career paths that suit you, and obtain a job where you will be happy and satisfied.

So – how do you find out more about yourself? You need to ask yourself some tough but important questions to identify your VIPS. We will show you how to do this and how to use self-assessment tools to help you with this process.

After completing my masters' degree in electrical engineering followed with three years of experience in the telecommunication industry as a technology consultant in my home country Serbia, I decided to start my MBA in Germany. I came to Germany not knowing that I would spend an amazing 18 months filled with many memorable situations.

One of the most valuable things for me was that I got a very clear understanding of myself. Doing self-reflection exercises, personality-assessments, and one-to-one coaching, I developed a good picture of my values, interests, personality, and skill set. I reviewed how I interact with people and identified how to evolve in the future.

Practising how to write a good résumé and cover letter, conducting mock interviews, and networking gave me a competitive edge when I started my job searching process. As part of my MBA thesis I did an internship with a large consulting company where I got the chance to apply everything that I learned during my studies. Studying for my MBA in Germany equipped me with the knowledge of how to approach and solve business problems in a structured and effective way, improved my soft skills, and enhanced my life experience. I am now working in one of the leading IT companies in the world and realized my dream!

Goran Popovic

These tools won't identify your dream career for you. Rather they will help you get a better idea of what is important to you, guide your job search and support you in evaluating options and making decisions. We will present some of these self-assessment tools later on in this chapter. You can check with your university's career office what tools they have and book an appointment to discuss your results.

The next four sections of this chapter take you on a journey to better understand your VIPS and how these apply to the transition from school to work. Let's begin with values.

Values

What is important to you? What do you care about? Is flexibility at work more important for you than salary? Is giving back to the community meaningful to you?

Values are the core beliefs that act as guideposts for our actions and priorities. Knowing your values can help you to identify the right career path and find a job which you truly enjoy. While values are relatively stable and enduring, nonetheless they do shift over time.

For example, as an international student currently looking for a job you might care more about money than work–life balance. This might change if you decide to start a family when you might value spending time with your children more than a high-paying job that requires extensive international travel. As such, reflect on your values once in a while because they act as a compass for you in setting goals and making decisions.[2]

Research has found that if an employee's values and personality align with an organization's culture the more likely it is that the employee is satisfied with his job. In such a situation, the employee is less likely to leave the organization and more committed to the organization. This is called person–organization fit.

For example, if you highly value creativity you might fit well with employers in industries such as media, advertising, and fashion. If you strongly value equality you might find it difficult to work for hierarchical organizations which value individual performance, such as financial institutions or sales related roles. You can complete online tests such as www.123test.com/work-values-test or www.onetcenter.org/WIL.html#overview. Alternatively, you can do the following exercise to identify your current set of values and how they guide you in finding the right work environment and job position.

From Table 6.1, choose the 10 values which you find most important. This is not a complete list of work related values; you can add others that you feel apply to you.

Once you have identified your key 10 values, rank them from 1 to 10. Then write down how you would define each value and provide an example whether each value has been met or not met in your past experience at school, at extra-curricular activities,

Intrinsic/personal values	Work content values	Work environment values	Work relationship values
Social recognition	Helping others	Predictability	Cultural diversity
Security	Chance to be creative	Quiet environment	Competitive relationships
Freedom	Intellectual stimulation	Safe environment	Cooperation/ collaboration
Equality	Precision work	Flexibility	Harmony
Honesty	Achievement focused	Pleasant surroundings	Support from supervisors/ colleagues
Power	Challenging work	High salary/ compensation	Open communication
Respect	High-risk work	Fast-paced	Trust
Sense of accomplishment	Detail-oriented work	Security	Recognition for achievements
Sense of belonging	Control of daily work	Lots of public contact	Autonomy
Integrity	Ability to see tangible results	Structure	Humor/fun

Table 6.1 Work-related values

or (if applicable) at work. Write down why you think that these values are important in your job search. Finally, ask close friends or classmates to check and comment. Keep your values in mind when you are searching for jobs and organizations to work for.

As you start to search and apply for jobs ask yourself the following questions in regard to potential employers and positions: To what extent are my own personal values reflected in the organization's values? Do my values converge, or diverge, from the organization's values? Is there a good fit between my values and those of the organization? Why so?

You might also draw on these values when you are thinking about questions to ask in the interview, such as the following:

- "Could you please describe the culture of your company?"
- "What do you like best about working in this organization?"
- "Is risk-taking encouraged and what happens when people fail?"

Interests

What do you enjoy? Which classes do you like most at university? Which hobbies do you have? Which extra-curricular activities give you energy? Do you enjoy activities which involve dealing with people more than activities which require technical skills? Which activities make you feel content and satisfied? Interests help you identify your ideal career. If you are deeply interested in what you do at work you are more likely to be successful and satisfied with your job.

Interests are different from skills. You may derive great pleasure from taking photographs, but may not be a skilled photographer. That is you have the interest, but not the skills. On the other hand, you might be really good at coding and computer languages but you actually don't like this activity very much. In other words, you have the skills but not the interest.

Once you understand your interests you can search for jobs and work environments that are more likely to satisfy you and make you happy. Based on psychologist John L. Holland's theory of vocational choice, you can identify your career interests and the work environment which fits you best.[3]

According to Holland's theory, people and work environments can be classified in six different groups. Depending on your personality and interests you prefer certain work environments over others. The six groups are: Realistic, Investigative, Artistic, Social,

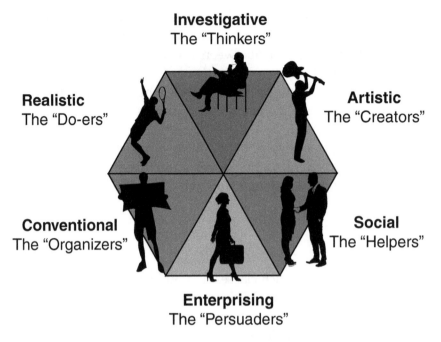

Figure 6.2 Holland or RIASEC groups

Enterprising, and Conventional (RIASEC). These are shown in Figure 6.2.

Most people will have the strongest career interest in two or three of these groups and that combination is called a RIASEC Code or Holland Code. Once you know your Holland code you can check the occupations list in Table 6.2 below to identify what careers match your interests.

> **TIP 6.1** Are you eager to conduct self-assessments using the Holland types? Here are two links to interest self-assessments https://openpsychometrics.org/tests/RIASEC (5–10 minutes to complete), and www.onetcenter.org/IP.html (10 minutes to complete).

Personality

How do you work? Do you prefer to lead or to follow? Do you prefer working alone or in teams? Do you make logical decisions or follow intuition? Do you prefer change over routine?

Holland type	Interests/likes	Occupation
Realistic	• Working with hands, tools and equipment; building things • Product-driven environments with clear lines of authority	Engineer, builder, technician, mechanic, electrician, computer technologist, aircraft controller, surveyor
Investigative	• Discovering and researching ideas, observing, investigating • Independent, unstructured working environments	Science, research, medical and health occupations; biologist, chemist, geologist, medical technologist
Artistic	• Performing, writing composing, designing • Self-expressive, unstructured work environments	Artist, architect, photographer, composer, singer, dancer, actor, reporter, editor, advertiser, fashion designer
Social	• Teaching, training, treating, caring, serving • Supportive, collaborative work environments	Instructor, nurse, counsellor, police officer, social worker, occupational therapist, customer service officer
Enterprising	• Leading, influencing, debating, selling • Fast-paced, entrepreneurial work environments	Salesperson, manager, management consultant, lawyer, politician, public relations specialist business owner, music or sports promoter
Conventional	• Organizing, planning, following procedures, working with data or numbers • Structured, organized, practical work environments	Financial officer, accountant, budget analyst, tax expert, statistician, librarian, paralegal, computer programmer

Table 6.2 Holland types with sample interests and occupations

Based on your personality you will prefer certain jobs over others. If there is a good fit between personality and your job, it is more likely that you are content and successful. This is called person–job fit.

Usually, people speak about personality in terms such as someone being dominant, talkative, open minded, shy, etc. These characteristics are called personality traits. They describe an individual's behaviour in a large number of situations.

Research has shown that humans can be portrayed along a few important personality traits. The two dominant frameworks for describing personality traits are the Myers–Briggs Type Indicator (MBTI) based on the theory of C. G. Jung, and the Five Factor Personality Model (the Big Five).[4] Both frameworks provide an assessment of your personality and will help you to gain more self-awareness and guide you in your career search.

The MBTI is the most widely used personality assessment in the world.[5] The indicator involves a series of situational questions with your answers categorized on four scales to determine your personality type.

1. **Extraverted or Introverted (E or I).**
   People scoring higher on the extraverted side of the scale tend to become energized by being around others. Introverts however get more energy from spending time by themselves. Extroverts are outgoing, social and assertive while introverts are more quiet and shy. Extroverts prefer to work in large groups rather than alone or in one-on-one situations like introverts.

2. **Sensing or Intuitive (S or N).**
   Sensing individuals are practical, enjoy order, and are detail oriented while intuitive people prefer to see the larger picture of life and rely on "gut" feelings. When making career decisions sensing types focus on job aspects such as benefits, location, and salary while intuition types are more interested in a job's potential.

3. **Thinking or Feeling (T or F).**
   This scale is important in decision-making: thinkers prefer reason and logic over emotions when making decisions.

Feelers on the other hand take emotion into consideration and identify with everyone involved when making decisions, whereas thinkers analyse the pros and cons of a situation objectively.

4. **Judging or Perceiving (J or P).**
   Judgers feel energized by getting things done. They are control-oriented, and enjoy structure and order. Perceivers are much more comfortable with last-minute pressures and are more flexible and spontaneous.

The first letters of the name of the dominant side of each scale (except that N is used for Intuitive) are combined to create a personality type. For example, ENTJ is a person who is extraverted, intuitive, thinking, and judging. This type of person is sometimes called "Commander" because they have a passion to lead others. ENTJ persons are best fitted in a job where they can address complex problems, be analytical and set clear goals, such as management consultant, lawyer, or financial analyst.

> **TIP 6.2** If you want to learn more about your personality type and which career might suit you best, you can use the following tests, based on Myers–Briggs and the Big Five: https://psychcentral.com/quizzes/personality-tests and www.16personalities.com

Skills

What are you good at? What things do you do well? What are your key abilities, talents, and strengths?

Identifying your key skills is important in making the right career choice. Assessing your skills and being able to communicate them will help you when writing résumés and cover letters and preparing to being interviewed.

In general, skills are learned behaviours and abilities which you have developed over time, and especially in school/university but also elsewhere (hobbies, volunteering, etc.). There are two sets of skills relevant for your career: hard or technical skills, and soft or transferable skills. Hard skills (or technical skills) are usually gained through formal training or education at school or university and can be measured or tested. Hard skills include knowledge of a specific subject: a language, computer software, chemical reactions, accounting standards, legal procedures, and many more.

For example, if you would like to become a marketing researcher you need to have factual knowledge of economic theories, survey methods, simulation and forecasting techniques as well as knowledge of principles and practices for determining consumers' wants and needs.

Soft skills are quite distinct from hard skills. Soft skills are those we use to interact with others and to approach life and work. Some examples of soft skills or transferable skills are oral communication and presentation skills, analytical and problem-solving skills, teamwork skills, etc.

Employers are not only looking for your knowledge and expertise in a certain area. A degree alone is not enough to convince employers that they should hire you. In fact, what is as important for them are the soft or transferable skills, which are desirable across industry sectors and job positions. As the name implies, these skills can be transferred from one job or context to another. You might have gained oral presentation skills in your courses by investing lots of time, and following the advice in Chapter 5. These skills were not only useful in your classes but you could also use the same communication skills in an internship and full-time job.

In fact, many of the skills you learned in the classroom are transferable ones: conducting research, summarizing information, reaching conclusions, working under time pressure, working in groups, taking notes, being creative, and much more.

As such it is important that you start reviewing and identifying your transferable skills – think about all the activities in your courses where you developed skills as well as extra-curricular activities, internships, and part-time jobs. The very fact that you are an international student will give you transferable skills, such as dealing positively with transitions and problem-solving!

To kick-start your thinking about your transferable skills consider the career readiness competencies for new college graduates that the National Association of Colleges and Employers in the USA has identified.[6] The eight career readiness competencies represent the skills, experiences, and attributes that students need in order to make a successful transition from university to employment:

1. **Critical thinking/problem-solving:** Exercise sound reasoning to analyse issues, make decisions, and overcome problems. The individual is able to obtain, interpret, and use knowledge, facts, and data in this process, and may demonstrate originality and inventiveness.

2. **Professionalism/work ethic:** Demonstrate personal accountability and effective work habits, e.g., punctuality, working productively with others, and time workload management. The individual demonstrates integrity and ethical behaviour, acts responsibly with the interests of the larger community in mind, and is able to learn from mistakes.

3. **Teamwork/collaboration:** Build collaborative relationships with colleagues and customers representing diverse cultures, races, ages, genders, religions, lifestyles, and viewpoints. The individual is able to work within a team structure, and can negotiate and manage conflict.

4. **Oral/written communications:** Articulate thoughts and ideas clearly and effectively in written and oral forms to persons inside and outside of the organization. The individual has public speaking skills; is able to express ideas to others; and can write/edit memos, letters, and complex technical reports clearly and effectively.

5. **Information technology application:** Select and use appropriate technology to accomplish a given task. The individual is also able to apply computing skills to solve problems.

6. **Leadership:** Leverage the strengths of others to achieve common goals, and use interpersonal skills to coach and develop others. The individual is able to assess and manage his/her emotions and those of others; use empathetic skills to guide and motivate; and organize, prioritize, and delegate work.

7. **Career management:** Identify and articulate one's skills, strengths, knowledge, and experiences relevant to career goals, and identify areas necessary for professional growth. The individual is able to explore job options, can take the

steps necessary to pursue opportunities, and can self-advocate for opportunities in the workplace.

8. **Global/intercultural fluency:** Value, respect, and learn from diverse cultures, races, ages, genders, sexual orientations, and religions. The individual demonstrates openness, inclusiveness, sensitivity, and the ability to interact respectfully with all people and understand individuals' differences.

As hopefully you can see, you've developed and improved all these skills in your studies. Some, such as global/intercultural fluency, you've mastered from being an international learner.

As an exercise, review each of the eight career competencies and write down where you have shown each one of them in the past. You could then rank the competencies from 1 (being poor) to 5 (being excellent). Highlight which of the competencies need further improvement and think about activities where you could develop these skills.

For example, if you rank your oral communication skills low, you might want to consider participating in activities which develop this skill. This can start with just asking a question in class, to becoming a member of the drama or debating club at your school; joining Toastmasters,[7] or just speaking more in a variety of situations.

Now that you've got a clear picture of your values, interests, personality, and skills (VIPS) you also have a clear picture of your potential career. You have successfully accomplished the first step in our career roadmap: knowing yourself!

TIP 6.3 Complete the Sokanu Career Test for more suggestions as to which careers might fit you. The test measures your values, interests, personality, skills, work style preferences, and salary expectations so as to suggest potential careers. You will need to answer 310 questions and it will take you 20–30 minutes to complete the test: www.sokanu.com.

Whatever self-assessments or career tests you do: remember that they are not prescriptive, they only provide you with ideas on careers you might want to consider and investigate further.[8] There is more to be done, as explained later in this chapter, to find your best path in the world of work.

Step 2: Market

The second step in our career roadmap is conducting in-depth research on potential careers – knowing the market. The market just means all the jobs and organizations that appeal to you and for which you are suited and qualified.

The market may be quite large for you if you consider three main employment sectors: private (for profit enterprises), public (governments and related organizations like the United Nations), not-for-profit/non-governmental sector (community agencies and many others). In addition, think about whether you would prefer to work in small or medium-sized companies, large corporations, or become self-employed.

As you narrow your potential career paths to match your VIPS you will want to find out more about the different jobs and organizations which interest you. You want to learn about job descriptions and labour market information such as employment outlook, salary and benefits, corporate culture, career progression, who has been hired in the recent past, the satisfaction of current employees, and much more. The more you know about the market, the more successful your job search will be.

You can start getting a better idea of different sectors, industries, and occupations by conducting "desk research." As the name desk research implies, you can investigate your potential career paths from the comfort of sitting behind a desk by browsing and searching various websites such as:

- *Job Bank* (Canada): This website published by the Canadian government provides information on different jobs, employment requirements, wages, and career prospects: www.jobbank.gc.ca/occupationsearch
- *Occupational Outlook* (USA): Information relating to the US labour market: www.bls.gov/ooh
- *Occupational Information Network O*Net* (USA): You can explore various occupations based on search criteria such as your skill set, required skills, high demand occupations, and related occupations: www.onetonline.org

- *Prospects* Job Profiles (UK): Useful information on job profiles in the UK: www.prospects.ac.uk/job-profiles
- Check your university career centre website for information on industries, job profiles, alumni stories, etc.
- Check company websites and search for videos as they can give you an insight into the organization, its employees, and its culture.

You may be surprised at the range of possible occupations and careers!

Based on your research, shortlist several occupations which you find interesting and then try to narrow it down to two or three occupations. Aim to have alternatives in place if your preferred option does not materialize, or if you realized that while you might be good at the skills required you wouldn't enjoy doing the job day in day out. Similarly, the job prospects might look quite gloomy or the average salary does not meet your expectations.

Don't get too stressed about coming up with two or three ideal occupations and workplaces. Rather, what is important is that you understand what is "out there" that suits and fits you.

Once you have identified the occupation which you are most interested in you need to search for open positions. You could start browsing through many websites which advertise thousands of job openings per day. This can be very time consuming and frustrating.

To make your job search more focused and efficient you could take the following approach.[9] First, create a list such as:

Employer	Job title/area of interest	Alumni/contact	Motivation

Spend 40 minutes searching for organizations that you find interesting (such as organizations you have always wanted to work for; employers you have found while searching job websites; and companies where your university's alumni/friends/family work). After exactly 40 minutes stop your company search – your first column should be filled with 40 employer names.[10]

Then, spend another 40 minutes to search for job titles areas of interest at these 40 companies. Stop again and fill in the second column. Then search for alumni or other potential contacts for another 40 minutes (use your university's alumni database, LinkedIn, and other sources). Spend the remaining time to think about how motivated you are for each position/company and rank them from 1 (being lowest) to 5 (being highest). Your employer target list could look like the following:

Company	Job title/area of interest	Alumni/contact	Motivation
AH company	Marketing Assistant	Yes	2
DEF company	Marketing	No	4
TMR company	Digitalization	Yes	5
....	...	...	...

Once you have created your company list, you can start your active job search phase. After having sat cozily behind your desk it is now time for you to meet people!

You might feel tempted to just simply send a standard résumé and cover letter to all the job openings which seem suitable. Based on our experience and that of many others, especially as an international student who might not have much work experience, this approach is not likely to be successful.

You have to take advantage of the so called "hidden job market." The majority of jobs are not actively advertised by organizations. By just submitting your applications to visible job adverts you are missing out on many job openings. You should therefore start to connect with people who work in your desired field to become aware of these hidden jobs and gain organization and industry knowledge. This networking approach is also called "informational networking."

Eventually, you might want to use the so called "advocacy networking" approach – knowing someone within your desired company who is willing to forward your application documents internally – a so called "referral." This will increase your chances that your application documents will actually land on the hiring manager's desk rather than being discharged earlier in the recruiting process. Some reports suggest that job applicants who are referred are three to four times more likely to be hired than someone who simply submits their application to the recruiter.

Informational networking

How do you find people who could provide valuable career insight, let you know about potential job openings, and could forward your application documents internally? What you need to do is network. This means that you connect with people to exchange information for mutual benefit and to create trusting professional relationships.

You might feel worried about the prospect of reaching out and connecting with people you don't know and have never met before. There are reasons for this: networking is not a common practice in your culture, you are uncomfortable due to your language skills, or you simply are a shy person.

From the moment I got off the plane from India, I was always told to increase my network. While I understood it, I didn't really *get* it. I felt that if I have the skills and potential, that should be enough. Probably an offshoot of my pride, or a byproduct of my culture, networking seemed like begging or fawning.

Despite my initial reservations about "wasting someone's time," I overcame my fears after a few meetings. I researched and got in touch with various hiring managers to speak to them about the skills they were looking for in potential employees.

I quickly realized that all people want something from each other: hiring managers want the right candidates, just as I want the right job. Therefore, a frank and mutual exchange of intention and interest is not unwelcome.

I now know networking is also learning: about people, organizations, and what is a right fit for me. Networking can be slow-going work but I kept on it. I understand now that networking is not groveling but rather connecting with people.

Shruti Ravuri

We don't suggest that you have to network in order to get an interview – it is just more likely that you will do so. Conducting informational interviews will also help you to get insight into the business culture of your host country – invaluable for an international student like you! Maybe you can overcome your reservations and try?

Here are five tips for building trusting professional relationships from which both parties benefit.

Networking takes time

In order to establish a professional relationship where the other party is willing to share her or his knowledge, experience and contacts will take time. Start networking three to six month before you actually think about submitting job applications. This means that if you are in a hurry to get a job you shouldn't start networking as your contacts will realize that you are desperate and only connecting with them because you want a job.[11]

Create and/or update your online presence

An online presence is useful to allow others to learn about you. LinkedIn, Facebook, and similar services and sites are increasingly essential for networking. We will walk you through the steps to do so on LinkedIn later in this chapter.

Prepare to tell your story

You need to be able to introduce yourself in a compelling and con-cise way. Review your VIPS to help you do so. This will be useful not only for conducting informational interviews but also for career fairs or other networking events.[12]

Depending on the situation you should be able to introduce yourself in 30 seconds ("elevator pitch") to around 3 minutes (at larger networking events). When you are asked who you are, state your name, where you originally come from, why you decided to become an international student, the name of your university and your field of study.

It is really powerful if you can mention that you have worked or are currently working on an academic project or assignment that is related to your desired career field. Include also, if possible, internship, work or volunteer experience, and highlight two to three skills or accomplishments. If time permits use the STAR technique (see Chapter 7) to outline your skills. Telling your story might sound easy – however, it takes time and effort to prepare a convincing introduction. Look back at Chapter 5 for tips on oral presentations.

Here is an example of a 30 second pitch from an international student:

> I'm Isabel Lopez. Two years ago, I moved from Venezuela to Seattle to study international relations at the University of Washington. I am passionate about improving the human rights situation of individuals worldwide. My experience as a volunteer at the Refugee Shelter has helped me to develop strong organizational skills, excellent listening skills and the ability to influence individuals. I am interested in broadening my experience in the human rights field and I would like to learn more about internship opportunities in your organization.

Create an overview of your existing contacts

Think about who you already know and create a spreadsheet: family, friends, former classmates, university peers, professors, mentors, members of religious or social groups, and people you know from extra-curricular activities (i.e. sports club, volunteering experience, etc.).

It will be much easier to reach out and talk to these people as you already have something in common with them. Your aim in getting in touch with them is to find out if they themselves work in your desired career field or if they know people who work in this field.

Create an overview of unknown contacts

Unknown contacts are those people who you don't know directly but with whom you share a common context, for example, a contact from a contact, an alumnus from your university whom you have found via your university's alumni association or on a social media platform such as LinkedIn, Facebook, or Twitter. An unknown contact can also be someone whose article you read, saw at a networking event, or was a guest speaker with whom you talked after your lecture, and so forth.

Setting up informational interviews

Once you have identified individuals (known or unknown) who work in your desired career field you need to set up informational interviews.

Normally, the initial contact for your unknown contacts is via email. However, you should always aim to eventually meet face to face. Try to keep your email brief and to the point, be polite, and proofread your text.

Here is a good email example for asking an alumna of your university for an informational interview. You can use a similar, but shorter text, to invite an alumna via LinkedIn or in other social media:

Subject line: Greetings from a student from your alma mater

Dear Ms. Wong,

I am an international student in the final year of my undergraduate English literature degree at La Trobe University. After graduation I am interested in starting a career in the publishing industry. Your profile and contact information is in the alumni directory of our university.

I would greatly appreciate the opportunity to speak with you to learn more about your experience in the publishing industry and your career path.

I would be extremely grateful if you could spare 15–20 minutes of your valuable time to speak with me within the next two weeks. Please let me know what dates and times suit you best.

Thank you very much in advance for your time and insight.

Sincerely yours,

Isabella Valez

[LinkedIn profile link]

Here is another example of how to ask for an informational interview:

Dear Mr. Karimi,

I attended your talk on "The blockchain transformation" in last week's supply chain management class. I found your insights on how blockchain is disrupting supply chain management extremely useful. In particular, I was fascinated by your company's effort to use blockchain to improve supply chain tracking.

As I plan to write my next assignment in my course on blockchain, I would be extremely grateful if I could ask you some more detailed questions. I am also keen to learn your perspectives about careers in the logistics industry.

Would you be available for a 20 minute phone or Skype call next week?

Sincerely yours,

Agniezska Nowicki

[LinkedIn profile link]

Don't get frustrated if you don't get a response from everyone after your first email. It might be the case that your message has been forgotten. You can send a friendly reminder after a couple of days, for example:

Dear Ms. Wong,

I hope that this email finds you well. I can only imagine how busy you are. I wrote you a couple of days ago regarding the possibility of asking you a few questions about your career path and experience in the publishing industry.

I would greatly appreciate it if you might be able to speak with me within the next few weeks.

Thank you very much in advance for your time and insight.

Sincerely yours,

Isabella Valez

[LinkedIn profile link]

If you don't get a response after the first reminder, stop contacting the person. Don't take the outcome personally – people are busy and sometimes simply just cannot respond. Keep your spirits up; your message to your next potential contact will be answered.

If the person does get back to you but is unable to speak with you, ask whether she or he could refer you to other people who might be able to help with your query.

Preparing and conducting informational interviews

Once you have arranged an informational interview, do spend some time researching more about the person you will be meeting. You can learn much on LinkedIn or similar websites, while also finding out as much as possible about the organization she or he works for. Think about good questions to ask which show your genuine interest in the person, occupation, and organization.

Figure 6.3 below shows you the kind of questions to ask during informational interviews. Adapt these questions to your interviews.

Questions about your contact person

I have read on your LinkedIn profile that ... why did you make this career move?

What skills are required in your position on a day-to-day basis?

What experiences best prepared you for where you are today?

What do you feel the most passionate about in your career?

Is there something you would wish somebody would have told you before choosing this career?

Questions about the industry

The industry has changed dramatically over the last years – how have you experienced it from inside?

I was reading in *journal x* that there is a trend towards y in your industry. What are your thoughts on this?

Figure 6.3 Informational interview questions

Who do you consider as competition for your organization?

What companies in this industry would you recommend me to research or investigate?

Where do you think this industry is heading?

Questions about the organization

What has changed about your organization in the last five years? How has that impacted how you approach your work?

What is the best/worst thing about your organization?

What are the biggest challenges that your organization is facing now?

What are potential career paths in your workplace?

What skills do really successful people have in your workplace?

Additional questions

What professional journals and associations have you found helpful?

Are there any other good resources to learn more about the industry?

What type of work samples or portfolio should I be trying to develop as I try to move into this career?

Do you have any recommendations of other people who I should talk to? Can I use your name when contacting them?

What next steps would you recommend for me?

Specific questions once you know the person better

What are the most effective strategies for seeking a position at this organization/in this career field?

What skills, experiences or personal attributes does your organization look for in new employees?

What profile do people have go get hired at my level?

Considering my background, how well do you think I would fit in your organization?

According to my research, the entry-level salary range for this job is usually in the range of … ? Does that match what you have seen?

Figure 6.3 (Cont.)

At this stage, it is all about gaining information and advice – do not ask whether there is a job available at the organization or whether your contact can refer you internally. Doing this places the person you are speaking to in an uncomfortable position, and destroys the trust you are aspiring to build. Your contact agreed to speak to you because you were not explicitly looking for a job in her or his organization. Once you have established a trusting relationship (remember, this takes time!) you might be able to ask these questions directly, or even better, your contact will offer this to you.

Send a thank you email to your interviewee no later than 24 hours after you have conducted the informational interview. Tell her or him how grateful you are for the support provided and share some key learning points which you gained from the meeting.

Here is a follow-up email example, shortly after an informational interview:

Subject line: Thank you

Dear Ms. Singh,

Thank you very much for taking the time to speak with me yesterday. I greatly benefitted from your insights into the pharmaceutical industry, particularly how your company is trying to switch from traditional marketing tactics to using more digital marketing.

Learning about your career path and your experiences in the pharma industry affirmed my wish to pursue a career in this area. I am extremely grateful for the contacts you have provided. I will reach out to them shortly and will keep you updated on my progress.

Again, thank you very much for your help.

Sincerely yours,

Eze Banjoko

[LinkedIn profile link]

After you have completed your informational interview, input information about this interview in a file to keep track of your contacts, including names and emails of contacts, interview date, topics discussed during the interview and insights gained. Recording this information will come in handy as you want to stay in touch with your contact.

A great way to keep in touch with your contact is to keep him or her informed about the meetings you've had with people your contact recommended. You can also let her or him know that the conversation inspired you to read a specific article or write an assignment for one of your classes. You can send your contact an article which you came across or the assignment that you wrote. You could also think about connecting him or her with people you have spoken to so they can increase their network as well. All of this will help you to build a positive and mutually beneficial relationship with your contact.

Building a network means keeping in touch with those you've interviewed. Four weeks after your informational interview, send a message like this one:

Subject line: Thank you

Dear Mr. Dixon,

Thank you again for sharing your advice and experience with me during our meeting on October 15th. I wanted to keep you updated on my progress on exploring the pharmaceutical industry.

As you suggested, I started reading *PharmaWeek* which helped me to learn more about the current trends in the pharma industry. I feel much more knowledgeable about the sector which led to a really engaging and meaningful meeting with Mr. Achebe who shared his company's approach to the increasing competition with me. Thank you very much for referring him to me.

Is there anyone else I should speak to or do you have further recommendations or suggestions?

Thank you again for your continuous support and please let me know if I can be of any assistance to you.

Sincerely yours,

Shivdeep Argarwal

[LinkedIn profile link]

Social media networking

Another way to learn more about your desired career path and get access to the hidden market is to engage in social media networking. This approach can be particularly useful for international students as you might feel more confident in using social media than in engaging with strangers via email.

The three most common social media networks in the Western world are LinkedIn, Twitter, and Facebook.

LinkedIn

LinkedIn gives you access to a huge professional network. You can find background information on potential interviewers and hiring managers on LinkedIn, which will help you to build rapport during job interviews. For example, you and your interviewee might have the same interests or previously lived in the same city or country.

You can not only find information on individuals on LinkedIn but also information on specific organizations. Read the "recent updates" section on the company's LinkedIn site to learn more about the organization's activities.

While you can search your university alumni database LinkedIn's alumni search tool allows you to easily identify and connect with alumni from your university. It is likely that the information on LinkedIn is more up to date than the university alumni database as alumni tend to be more inclined to update their LinkedIn profile.

LinkedIn allows you to search for jobs using filters such as experience level, job function, company, industry, location, and many more. Likewise, companies are searching for candidates on LinkedIn so you shouldn't miss out on the opportunity to create your personal brand and to highlight your skills and experience.

Twitter

While Twitter is not a networking tool such as LinkedIn or Facebook, it is a micro-blogging site which offers you the opportunity to search for company related information (which will help you to answer interview questions such as "Why do you want to work for our company?").

You can search for job vacancies by using the hashtag #job and typing in your desired job, industry, and location. If you want to learn more about a specific company or industry you can simply "follow" the company or industry news to receive the latest information. This shows that you are interested and trying to keep abreast with recent developments in your desired company and/or industry.

Facebook

Unlike LinkedIn, which is mainly a professional networking tool, Facebook is more tailored to connect with family and friends. When recruiters are searching for potential candidates they will also check candidates' online presence. You therefore need to ensure that your party pictures and cartoon avatars stay private by setting your privacy settings accordingly.

Similar to LinkedIn and Twitter you can find company information on Facebook. Many companies post their jobs on their Facebook company page, provide videos of current employees who share their inside view of the company, or promote upcoming events.

Using LinkedIn as an international student

How do you create a great LinkedIn student profile, showcasing your unique experiences and professional interests? How do you use LinkedIn to network and find jobs?

Select a professional photo

If you want to increase your chances of being found by recruiters, and getting invites to connect with, you need to make sure that your profile includes a professional photo.

According to LinkedIn, your profile will be viewed seven more times if it includes a photo! You should therefore select a high-quality photo of you alone, preferably a head-shot, which shows you in professional attire and is up to date.

Use a captivating headline

There are thousands of student profiles on LinkedIn, many of them with a similar headline using just one-word like "student" or "undergrad student" without any additional information. Use the headline space to create a short, memorable professional slogan. State what you do and what you want to do.

Here are some good examples for a catchy headline: "High performing recent Fine Arts graduate – excellent writer and communicator" or "English and Sociology graduate seeking position with sustainability start-up," "International student graduating with BA – Ready to Tackle Poverty," or "Undergraduate student: Electrical Engineering and Renewable Energies."

Write a convincing summary

This section will need most of your attention and time. Crafting a compelling LinkedIn summary statement is a challenge – but it is worth it. Doing so gives you the chance to highlight your experiences, skills, and motivation. Treat it like drafting the first paragraphs of a cover letter (for more information on cover letters see Chapter 7). Rather than simply reciting your résumé, your summary should tell a story about you and your career aspirations.

- Write in the first person – a story about you and not a third person.
- Keep it brief – around three to four paragraphs.
- Try to grab the reader's attention by providing evidence for your interests, motivation, skills, and career aspirations. Highlight quantifiable or relevant achievements gained from

class assignments, presentations, and projects; during work or internship experience; extra-curricular activities; and elsewhere.

- Include keywords as recruiters are searching for potential candidates by filtering for specific keywords. Don't list your key skills, instead, include them in your story.
- Avoid using buzzwords such as driven, motivated, innovative, results-oriented, dynamic, team player, etc.
- If you are experiencing a hard time writing your summary, check out profiles of alumni or other professionals who are working in your desired career field to get inspired. Identify how they present themselves and what keywords and skills they highlight. Adjust your profile summary accordingly.
- Proof-read your summary and check for typos and grammar errors. Your LinkedIn profile is accessible to everyone on LinkedIn, so make sure that you create a professional image of yourself.

Here's an example of a well written LinkedIn student summary:

> I am currently in my final year of a Bachelor of Fine Arts in the School of Drama at Carnegie Mellon University with an emphasis on stage and production management. My enthusiasm for theatre began at my high school in Spain where I was the producer for two years of my high school's annual play, which was awarded first prize (out of 22 plays) in the region of Murcia.
>
> I decided to pursue my university studies as an international student in America due to my intense interest in 20th century American theatre, and the best place to learn more was at Carnegie Mellon University. Last summer, I interned at La Jolla Playhouse learning customer service skills and increasing my understanding of how a facility that houses performing arts events is run.

Over the last two years I have been the head of the student drama society at my university organizing rehearsals and communicating with all parties involved, including actors and the creative team.

I plan to become a successful theatre manager combining my passion for the theatre with my organizational and people skills.

Fill in the remaining boxes

Current position

This is the section where you should put in where you currently work and what your achievements and results are. If you currently have a part-time job or are doing an internship you can include this information here. Don't just list your job duties, people are much more interested to learn about how you perform in the job.

If you are currently not working leave this box blank.

Industry

You can add what industry you are interested in. Choose the closest match to your desired industry. If you are unsure in which industry you would like to work, leave this box blank.

Education

This section is important as it tells readers that you either already have received a university degree or are expecting to graduate at a specific time. Include all relevant degrees (undergraduate and graduate) you received or are expecting to receive, including the institutions. This will enable you to network and connect easily with alumni of these institutions.

Country, postal code, and locations within this area

Here you can put in your location. The more information you provide, the more tailored offers LinkedIn can provide you with, such as job or internship opportunities with the area, joining local groups, etc. A word on privacy: LinkedIn won't show your postal code on your public profile. Check your privacy settings for more details.

Experience

The experience section in your LinkedIn profile is as essential as it is in your résumé (see Chapter 7 for more information on résumés). Don't get stressed about the fact that you might not have much experience to add in this section – you are an international student so no one expects you to have extensive work experience.

However, you might have done internships (paid and unpaid), part-time jobs, or entrepreneurial or freelance work which you could include. List your jobs and internships in chronological order, starting with the most recent. Similar to the current position box: Don't just simply state your job duties, rather focus on your accomplishments.

Skills

Remember what your VIPS are? Having already reflected upon your skills in the "me" section earlier in this chapter will now make it easier for you to add the relevant skills to your LinkedIn profile.

Check out which skills listed in job descriptions appeal to you and search for profiles of people who are working in your desired career field and note what skills they have ticked. Ensure that you can always provide evidence for the skills which you are stating.

Contact and personal info

Similar to the country, postal code, and location section on LinkedIn you can decide what information you want to make available to whom. If you want that only your 1st connections (people you are directly connected with) can see your email or phone number set your settings accordingly.

Volunteer experience

This is a great section, especially for you as an international student who might not have much work experience but more volunteering experience. Don't just state your volunteering experience. Include what transferable skills you have gained and what results you have achieved.

Accomplishments

This is another useful section for you as you can highlight achievements such as honours and awards you have received, projects successfully undertaken, courses you have completed (not your credit bearing courses but online courses that you have completed in your spare time, for example EdX, Coursera, etc.).

List any professional certifications you have gained and those languages which you are speaking on a more than basic conversational level. You can also add any publications – be it a piece you have written for a university publication, a paper you have written for an academic or practitioner journal, or an online contribution.

Stating your membership in professional organizations, university clubs, and societies can also be beneficial as you could connect and relate much easier to someone (such as a recruiter or hiring manager) who has also been in the same organizations.

Recommendations

Think about who in your network could recommend you and your work: your professors, classmates, mentors, the people who wrote letters of reference for you in the past, co-workers, and others. Ask them to write a few lines for you. Recommendations can be extremely powerful as they provide evidence for recruiters and your connections that you are credible.

Add examples of your work

Another way of demonstrating your skills is to share your work. You can add assignments for courses, group presentations, and other work you have done for your studies.

More LinkedIn features

Connect with people

LinkedIn has useful features that allow you to easily network once you have created your own profile. At first, start connecting with people you know such as your family, friends, classmates from high school, current classmates at university, people you know from extra-curricular activities or volunteer work, previous managers at work, co-workers, and professors. You can then begin to reach out to people you don't know. Make sure that you personalize your invitation to enhance your chances that your request gets accepted.

After graduating as an international student, I wanted to work for a healthcare company or in a top consulting firm.

What made this happen for me was doing a lot of research on LinkedIn. I noted the background of the people who were in my preferred industry and contacted some for pointers to help me as a newbie in the industry. I never asked for a job!

Furthermore, I talked to alumni. I used career events to speak to the industry experts to obtain their insights. I followed up with them after the event if we had an interesting discussion during the event.

Lastly, I decided to do an internship to get a head start into the corporate culture and have my foot in the door for full-time employment. I am now working as a consultant in the healthcare industry.

Vivek Singh

Join groups

Make an effort to join groups for students or alumni or professional communities which represent your desired career goal. Be sure to update your status on a regular basis, posting projects you are working on, events you are attending or books and articles you have read and found useful. This will help to boost your professional image.

LinkedIn samples

To help you with preparing your LinkedIn profile, we've got a sample to share with you. Here is the profile of a recent international student graduate:

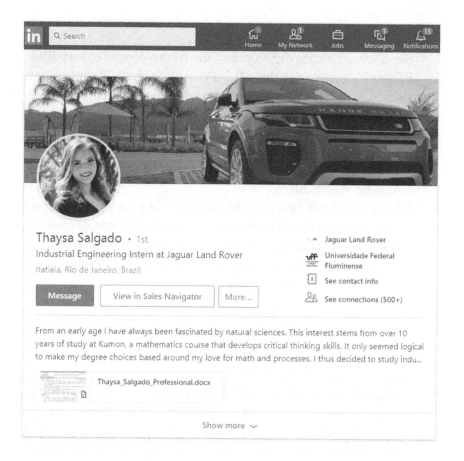

You can find many more examples and adopt the elements that best showcase your background, education, and skills.

Lets recap...

Having followed the first two steps of the Triple M Career Roadmap you have identified the values, interests, personality, and skills (VIPS) that will shape your career. You've also learned about what employment opportunities there are for you, and built a network of people already working.

The next step is to apply for jobs. For this you need an exceptional résumé. The next chapter shows you how to write one.

Notes

1   See www.weforum.org/reports/the-future-of-jobs-report-2018

2   Edgar H. Schein, at the MIT Sloan School of Management, studies how the self-image of an individual's values, motives, and competency can act as guiding principles in making career choices. If you want to learn more and do a self-assessment, please see Edward H. Schein and John Van Maanen, *Career Anchors: The Changing Nature of Work and Careers* (San Francisco, CA: John Wiley, 2016).

3   John L. Holland (1919–2008) was an American psychologist who first wrote about how people should make career choices. His last book is *Making Vocational Choices: A Theory of Vocational Personalities and Work Environments* (Odessa, FL: Psychological Assessment Resources, 1997).

4   Robert R. McCrae and Paul T. Costa, Jr., "Toward a New Generation of Personality Theories: Theoretical Contexts for the Five-Factor Model," in Jerry S. Wiggins, ed. *The Five-Factor Model of Personality: Theoretical Perspectives* (New York: Guilford, 1996), 51–87.

5   Katharine Cook Briggs (1875–1968) with her daughter Isabel Briggs Myers (1897–1980) developed the Myers–Briggs Type Indicator (MBTI). Neither was a professor or formal researcher. See Merve Emre, *The Personality Brokers: The Strange History of Myers-Briggs and the Birth of Personality Testing* (New York: Penguin Random House, 2018).

6   The list of career readiness competencies in this book, is taken with some editing, from the American National Association of Colleges and Employers, found at www.naceweb.org/career-readiness/competencies/career-readiness-defined

7   See www.toastmasters.org

8   If you are still struggling to identify which career path is the right one for you, check out Bill Burnett and Dave Evans, *Designing your Life: How to Build a Well-Lived, Joyful Life* (New York: Alfred A. Knopf, 2016).

9   See Steve Dalton, *The 2-Hour Job Search: Using Technology to Get the Right Job Faster* (New York: Random House, 2012). Dalton is the Program Director for Daytime Career Services at the

Fuqua School of Business at Duke University. You can connect with him at: www.linkedin.com/in/2hourjobsearch/

10   If you are looking for jobs in the Western world you could check out job boards such as Monster, Dice, or CareerBuilder or use job search engines such as Indeed.com or Glassdoor which aggregate information from job boards and company websites as well as provide you with company reviews and company-specific salary data. Speak with career advisers at your university to find out what country-specific job boards or search engines they recommend.

11   See Adam Grant, *Give and Take: Why Helping Others Drives Our Success* (New York: Penguin Books, 2014). In this award-winning book Grant explains that successful individuals are those people who give more than they take. This is especially relevant when networking with others.

12   Career and job search coaches Nathan Perez and Marcia Ballinger developed a model on how to successfully network. See Nathan A. Perez and Marcia Ballinger, *The 20-Minute Networking Meeting* (Minneapolis, MN: Career Innovation Press, 2012).

Match (I)
The résumé

Luck is what happens when preparation meets opportunity.

Seneca

Introduction

For the vast majority of students writing a résumé is not an exciting task. You may procrastinate when composing your résumé because it is daunting and you're not sure how to do it. After all, how can one summarize education, relevant skills, experiences, and accomplishments in just one or two pages? Or you may feel that writing your résumé is easy and won't need much time and effort. You can just pull it together whenever you need it.

International students face more hurdles than other students in composing their résumés. This is because your path to graduation might have been different than other students, or perhaps you have specific skills (like languages) that other students don't have. Highlighting the value of an international education can be difficult on a résumé or in a cover letter.

The importance of résumés

Creating your résumé should be your top priority as it will be your golden ticket to landing an interview at your dream job. Did you know that large companies like Google receive over 5,000 applications per day? On average, good job openings in the public and private sectors attract 250 résumés.

Of these hundreds of applicants, four to six will be called for an interview and only one will be offered the job. We do not want to scare you with this information, however, we want to raise your awareness of how important résumé writing is. You need to make sure that your résumé stands out and is placed on the top of the stack, especially since recruiters spend only around six seconds looking at each résumé.

The current digital era makes it even more complicated. Most large corporations utilize applicant tracking systems (ATS). ATS scan résumés to filter irrelevant applications by matching the terms used in your résumé with those in the job description. This process results in up to 75 per cent of résumés being rejected before the recruiter or hiring manager even sees them.

We will make writing a résumé a less frustrating task for you by providing you with advice based on our experience working with many different types of international students. We want to motivate you to take an early, pro-active role in preparing your résumé so that it opens doors for interviews. As an international student, or someone about to apply for international study, you already know that a résumé is pretty important. This is because some study abroad and exchange application procedures require a résumé.

What follows is geared for international students looking for employment. However, the same advice and guidelines apply if you require a résumé for another purpose.

The value of a résumé

You may wonder why résumés are so important. After all, you have your transcript from your studies listing your courses and grades? Will that not be enough for an employer to decide whether to interview you?

A résumé is your professional calling card. It tells much more about who you are and what you can do than a transcript. The résumé goes far beyond the grades you've earned in the class-room to include your skills, achievements, and character. The very format of a résumé is informative for potential employers. A well-organized résumé suggests a logical and efficient person. An actively worded résumé implies a proactive individual.

Like the statement of interest (Chapter 2) a good résumé is very hard to write. Indeed, your résumé is among the hardest of documents you'll ever compose. After all, you are a complex and multifaceted person. How to summarize you in a page or two? Doing it well will require every writing and thinking skill you have.[1]

A terrific résumé is one that after being read makes the reader exclaim, "I know this person. I can tell what she'll be like at work!"

Create a simple and clean résumé layout

Think of the résumé as a passport. All passports, regardless of country, have the same format. This allows for border officials to quickly find the information that is needed about you. The same applies for résumés.

To make sure that your résumé passes the applicant tracking system (ATS) and catches the recruiter's interest it needs to follow a certain layout and formatting and must be easy to read. Some ATS have problems with certain formatting and fonts so you have to write your résumé to be ATS-friendly. Even without the ATS, you want a résumé that is clear and easy to read, and follows the expected format.

There is software that allows you to conduct your own ATS analysis. VMock is a very useful tool for checking your résumé. It focuses on basic formatting standards and the way your experience is presented. Give it a try at www.vmock.com

Jobscan checks how well your résumé is tailored for the job you are applying for. First, you upload your résumé and the job description. Jobscan then checks how your résumé matches the keywords and phrases in the job description. The Jobscan software even offers you advice on how to better optimize your résumé for an ATS by providing examples and alternative suggestions. Access it at www.jobscan.co

Once you have passed the first technical hurdle, you need to impress the recruiter. Put yourself in the shoes of recruiters: they want to see within a very short period of time whether you might be the right candidate for the job and how you could add value to the organization.

You quickly need to get across your key characteristics and skills such as your unique experiences, qualifications, and personality. If recruiters can't easily find the relevant information in your résumé you will not be selected for an interview.

As a general guideline, you should lay out your résumé as follows:

- Black and white, with a minimum size 10 sans-serif font such as Calibri or Tahoma.
- Use standard one inch margins.
- Use bullet points.
- Avoid using tables, graphics, or logos.
- One page for employers in the USA, Canada, and UK, with two pages allowed for applicants with extensive experience.
- Check spelling and grammar.

The above refers mainly to the USA, Canada, and the UK. If you intend to apply for a job in other countries you need to adhere to the specific requirements there.[2] Recruiters' perspectives on how résumés should look vary significantly from country to country.

Table 7.1 below summarizes the general differences between the USA, Canada, and the UK, and other countries. Note, however, that this is a general summary, and that each country has its own particular standards and traditions in regard to résumés, and that job application requirements change over time.

To help you prepare your résumé and show you the regional differences, we have included five sample résumés later in this chapter.

Tailor your résumé to the job you are applying for

Recruiters use ATS to identify relevant applications from irrelevant applications. The ATS scans the application for the specific keywords that the recruiter programmed in advance. If your

	USA, Canada, UK	Rest of the world
Number of pages	1 (2 in some cases)	2–4
Photo	No	Yes
Contact detail/ personal information	Does not include date of birth, marital status or immigration status	Sometimes includes date of birth, marital status and/or immigration status
Educational information	Does not include high school Does not include TOEFL or SAT scores	Sometimes includes high school Includes TOEFL and/or SAT/GMAT scores
Date and signature	Does not include date and signature	Sometimes includes date and signature

Table 7.1 Requirements for résumés: USA, Canada, UK, and rest of the world

résumé matches the recruiter's pre-defined requirements (i.e. the right keywords and phrases), it will then land on the recruiter's desk or screen to be reviewed. This means that your résumé needs to be carefully tailored for each and every job you are applying for.

Every time you apply for a job at a certain company, you need to re-write and adjust your résumé. You need to dissect each job description and identify those skills and experiences which the recruiter is looking for. Does this sound tedious to you? Based on our experience, this is the most valuable time you can spend in ensuring that your résumé gets you an interview.

I always intended not only to study abroad but also to live and work abroad. I was successful in my school application and started studying full of enthusiasm.

Once I graduated, I expected that finding a job would be not too difficult. Surely, recruiters would value my acquired knowledge. However, this proved to be wrong.

Initially all my applications were met with rejection. It was an emotional roller-coaster ride for me. Eventually I realized that I had to spend considerably more time in preparing my application documents such as my résumé and cover letter.

In order to outshine other candidates I began to tailor my résumé to the job requirements and the specific standards of the country. In my case, I had to include my picture, use many action verbs, and prove to the employer that I had potential and would add value to the organization.

After making changes in my résumé my success rate started to improve and soon I was able to land a job of my liking.

Suramya Tyagi

To make life easier for you, you might want to create a standard résumé first which includes all your past experience, including work-related jobs, coursework, projects, extra-curricular experiences, and any awards or special recognition you may have received. Put the job description next to your standard résumé and circle the experiences, qualifications, and skills in your standard résumé which match the requirements outlined in the job description. Copy and paste the circled items into your tailored résumé. Try to use the same language in your tailored résumé as the job description. Identify the keywords used in the job description and try to incorporate them in your tailored résumé.

How a standard résumé should be structured and what it should include is summarized in Table 7.2. The standard résumé is one that includes everything that could possibly appear in your résumé. As such, it will be much longer than the tailored résumé you submit to a potential employer.

Using the best action words

In your standard résumé, and then in the shorter tailored version that you prepare for submission, you must use action words. These

Contact details	• Full name • Mobile number, mailing address, and email • Links to personal website, blog, or LinkedIn profile
Key skills	• Highlight your best four to eight qualifications/skills that make you a good candidate for the job
Education	• Highest degree first, name of degree first then name of school • Include honours and awards received, e.g. "Ranked 5 out of 100 students" or "graduated with honours" • Include your GPA, such as 3.2/4
Coursework/ projects/ assignments	• Include course assignments and projects that demonstrate the skills laid out in the job description • Describe your contributions and accomplishments rather than focusing on a description of the project itself • Include reports or assignments you've written, presentations prepared, case studies, book reviews, and other course work • Highlight teamwork and projects done in collaboration with other students • Use past tense and active voice when stating things that are not occurring in the present
Work experience	• Relevant work experiences in reverse chronological order • List name of employers, dates of employment, positions you held and bulleted list of responsibilities and achievements • Specify and quantify your tasks where possible, e.g. supported weekly meetings for five departments • Include accomplishments, achievements, and recognition received when stating job tasks • Provide background information on less well-known employers, e.g. number of employees, to give the recruiter a better idea of the company • If possible, job titles should match the ones stated in the job description. You can tweak the titles at previous companies to more closely match the new job you are applying for
Extra-curricular/ positions/ awards/ scholarships/ certifications	• Leadership or other roles at student initiatives • Volunteering • Sports when played competitively and/or when holding positions of responsibility, such as coaching

Table 7.2 Standard résumé structure

words are at the core of a strong résumé, as they demonstrate you are a proactive and high performing individual, who has a set of accomplishments. In Table 7.3 is a list of action verbs to describe your tasks and accomplishments. Avoid over-using the same word by using the synonyms that we've provided.

Résumé samples

This section shows you résumés of international students. The first two résumés are of international bachelor graduates applying for a position in Canada. The third example illustrates a résumé of an international master student applying for a position in the USA, and the fourth clarifies how to apply for a position in Germany as an international MBA student. The very last résumé shows you a résumé which lacks some major requirements and needs considerable further improvement.

Let's start with Figure 7.1, which is an annotated résumé of an international bachelor student applying for an entry-level marketing position in a Canadian company with subsidiaries in South Africa. Would you call him for an interview after seeing his résumé? Why?

Figure 7.2 is the résumé of an international bachelor graduate applying for a games developer job in Canada. Again, is this someone you would wish to hire? Why?

> **TIP 7.1** Use the email address provided by your university if possible, not gmail or others. This highlights that you are a student, or recently have been one. Don't use cute or personal email addresses like "snowinjune@gmail" or "babeinwonderland@mymail"

The next résumé, in Figure 7.3, is of an international student who is completing a Master's degree and applying for an engineering position in the USA.

Next in Figure 7.4 is the résumé for an international MBA graduate applying for a corporate transaction manager position in Germany. Note how the format of the résumé is different. Note also how the résumé writer, who has no previous employment experience in Germany, has crafted their résumé to be as accessible as possible for German employers.

Finally, in Figure 7.5, we have a poor résumé. What makes this a weak résumé? How would you improve it?

Analytical

analysed	determined	investigated	recommended
assessed	estimated	measured	researched
compared	evaluated	negotiated	studied

Communication

authored	edited	reported	translated
drafted	presented	summarized	wrote

Creativity

constructed	envisioned	illustrated	shaped
designed	fabricated	produced	visualized

Flexibility

adapted	amended	converted	improvised
adjusted	altered	grew	tailored

Initiative

advanced	demonstrated	implemented	revised
coordinated	established	launched	suggested

Leadership

advised	delegated	fostered	led
allocated	directed	hired	motivated

Organization

arranged	collected	organized	recorded
centralized	compiled	planned	scheduled

Problem-solving

customized	identified	rectified	restored
extended	reconciled	remodeled	streamlined

Teamwork

assisted	contributed	mediated	partnered
collaborated	cooperated	participated	shared

Additional action verbs

added	involved	prepared	secured
executed	maintained	measured	submitted
familiarized	performed	reviewed	transmitted

Table 7.3 Action words for use in résumés

JAMIE VAN VUUREN
Birch Street 58, Vancouver, Canada, V3X 5H7
jvanvuuren@unimail.com, +1 (123) 456-7777
LinkedIn.com/in/jvuuren

EDUCATION

09/2015-expected graduation 11/2019	**University of British Columbia, Vancouver, Canada** Bachelor of Arts, Double Major: Journalism and Creative Writing; Minor: German Overall GPA: 3.6, Honors each semester

KEY SKILLS

- Proficient in MS Word, Excel, Powerpoint, Adobe Photoshop
- Salesforce experience
- Fluent in Afrikaans and German

- Excellent customer service and communication skills as exemplified by Employee of the Year award
- Analytical skills as shown in social media research project

WORK EXPERIENCE

11/2018–Present   **Library Assistant | University of British Columbia, Vancouver**
- Advise students regarding reference-questions and database searching
- Wrote blog entry for undergraduate students on how to effectively use library
- Won Outstanding Student Employee of the Year award due to excellent customer service and research skills

07/2018–09/2018   **Program Assistant | University of British Columbia, Vancouver**
- Provided editing, copying and typing support to eight program managers
- Prepared and coordinated four information sessions
- Analyzed data for statistical purposes

07/2017–09/2017   **Marketing Intern | Marketing Global, Los Angeles, USA**
- Produced promotional material which was praised by supervisor as "innovative and focused on target audience"
- Performed market research through interviews and focus groups
- Managed Customer Relationship Management database

RELEVANT COURSEWORK

01/2019–03/2019   **Social Media Research Group Project | The Edge, Vancouver, Canada**
- Conducted secondary research on the definition and demographic use of social media data

EXTRA-CURRICULAR ACTIVITIES

01/2017–01/2018   **Head of Marketing | Entrepreneurship Club | University of British Columbia, Vancouver**
- Planned and ran five events with up to 200 participants
- Created LinkedIn Group page, growing engagement by club members by 10%

09/2014–10/2016   **Student Mentor | Keele Elementary School, Vancouver**
- Mentored 8th grade students, assisted with high school applications, readings and assignments

Figure 7.1 Sample résumé 1

Xiu Ying (Sally) Zhang

King Street 78, Vancouver, Canada, V3X 5H7
xiuyingzhang@unimail.com, +1 (555) 789-1967
LinkedIn.com/in/Xiuyingzhang

EDUCATION

09/2014–11/2018	**University of British Columbia, Vancouver, Canada** Bachelor of Science, Computer Science for Games Development, Graduated cum laude
09/2016–09/2017	**Shanghai Science School, Shanghai, China** • 12-months Study Abroad at #1 ranked university for Computer Science in China • Exercised problem solving skills in navigating new setting

KEY SKILLS

- Advanced user of 2D/3D modelling and animation software
- Experienced user of C++ and C#
- Fluent in English and Chinese Mandarin

- Outstanding technical and analytical ability
- Excellent team working skills and ability to work independently as shown in final year project
- Strong intercultural skills as lived and studied in two different countries

RELATED COURSEWORK

Virtual Environments, Multiplayer Game Development, Advanced Mobile Application Development
Final year project:
- Developed design, generated script/storyboard, and created visual aspects for new game "Ultimate Kingdom"
- Produced "Ultimate Kingdom" by incorporating previous study material and learning Unity 3D from scratch
- Received "Best Final Year Project Award"

EXTRA-CURRICULAR ACTIVITIES

10/2017–11/2018	**Founder and Head of Game Developer Club	University of British Columbia, Vancouver, Canada** • Created and initiated new student club in first year of study • Grew membership base by over 60% within last two years • Established industry network with over 20 companies across Canada to showcase student work
01/2014–09/2015	**Captain	Girls Volleyball Team	University of British Columbia, Vancouver, Canada** • Led team to win last year's national university competition • Effectively communicated with a diverse group of athletes and coaches

Figure 7.2 Sample résumé 2

Jorge Vargas
Close Street 22, Tuscaloosa, USA, 22012
lvargas@unimail.com, +1 (111) 442 8899
LinkedIn.com/in/jorgevargas

EDUCATION

09/2018-expected graduation 09/2019	**University of Alabama, Tuscaloosa, USA** MSc Operations Management Current Overall GPA: 3.3/4
09/2013-09/2017	**University of Chile, Santiago, Chile** BSc in Mechanical Engineering Overall GPA: 3.2/4, Franklin Scholarship

KEY SKILLS

- Demonstrated analytical skills and affinity for processes as Logistics Engineer Assistant
- Excellent intercultural and perseverance skills acquired from living and studying in two different countries
- Strong communication and interpersonal skills during volunteering experience as Math Tutor and President of the Hispanic Student Organization
- Advanced knowledge of MATLAB, Microsoft Excel/Access
- Language fluency: Spanish (native), English (fluent)

WORK EXPERIENCE

10/2017-06/2018	**Corporation El Naval, Santiago, Chile** Logistics Engineer Assistant - Analysed best balance between service level, transport costs and inventory levels using scientific and mathematical models - Arranged shipments placed by the Procurement Department and assured timely delivery - Coordinated quality inspections for import process in supplier facilities
01/2015-02/2015	**Grupo Donaso, Santiago, Chile** Retail Assistant, Intern - Managed payments and obtained documents required - Cooperated with internal and external stakeholders to ensure demands and needs of customers were met

EXTRA-CURRICULAR ACTIVITIES

10/2018-present	**President Hispanic Student Organization	University of Alabama, Tuscaloosa, USA** - Led monthly meetings and represented the organization to the university - Planned and organized social events with up to 200 attendees to draw awareness to and educate college community about Hispanic cultures
02/2014-06/2016	**Volunteer Math Tutor	Colegio Internacional, Santiago, Chile** - Tutored 12 elementary school children in math on a weekly basis - Developed tools and exercises to teach the importance of careful reasoning

Figure 7.3 Sample résumé 3

Tashmina Nawab

Höherstraße 1, 40625 Düsseldorf
tnawab@unimail.com, 0156 456 789
LinkedIn.com/in/tashminanawab

Photo

Date of Birth: 13/03/1991
Nationality: Pakistani

EDUCATION

09/2016- 09/2017	**WHU – Otto Beisheim School of Management, Düsseldorf, Germany** Master of Business Administration (MBA) with international modules in: Kellogg School of Management (Northwestern University), Chicago, USA Indian Institute of Management Bangalore (IIMB), Bangalore, India China Europe International Business School (CEIBS), Shanghai, China Overall GPA: 3.7 out of 4.0 (German equivalent 1.0) Master Thesis topic: Ethical challenges in corporate transactions
09/2009- 09/2012	**University of London, Affiliated Program Lahore, Pakistan** Bachelor of Laws (LL.B.Hons.), Specialization: Corporate Law Overall GPA: 3.8 out of 4.0 (German equivalent 1.3)
09/2009	**Fairfield High School, Lahore, Pakistan** High School Diploma, Overall GPA: 3.8 out of 4.0 (German equivalent 1.0)

WORK EXPERIENCE

01/2014- 05/2016	**Faisal Law Associates, Lahore, Pakistan** Legal Services, Associate - Dealt with joint ventures and acquisition proceedings - Led audit team and conducted annual legal audits for financial institutions
10/2012- 12/2013	**Dalir Textile Ltd., Lahore, Pakistan** Retail Industry, Legal Officer - Liaised with new companies and ensured compliance with regulations - Handled legal concerns and compiled legal reports

INTERNSHIPS

06/2011- 09/2011	**Square Partners, Lahore, Pakistan** Consulting, Intern - Conducted feasibility study for international development projects and financial due diligences

EXTRA-CURRICULAR ACTIVITIES

09/2016- 09/2017	**WHU-Otto Beisheim School of Management** MBA Class Speaker - Initiated and organized quarterly MBA Nights in collaboration with program office and fellow students to enhance campus experience
01/2010- 01/2012	**KBC Association, Lahore, Pakistan** Media, Volunteer Writer - Covered current affairs focusing on Asia

LANGUAGE AND COMPUTER SKILLS

Languages: Urdu (native), English (fluent, TOEFL score: 100), German (basic, A2)
IT Skills: Solid understanding of Microsoft Office

Düsseldorf, 15/10/2019

Tashima Nawab

Figure 7.4 Sample résumé 4

Jonny Miller

University Road 1111, Vancouver, Canada, V3X 5H7

joedoe@hotmail.com

Key Skills/Traits

Computer Skills, Detail-oriented, Passionate, Team Playr, Good communicator

Education:

University of Vancouver (2017), GPA 3.0

Experience:

FRK, Sales Assistant, Vancouver, Canada

I worked for six weeks at FRK and helped to sell products to customers. I was responsible for the display of products, checking inventory and assuring that ETPR requirements are met.

2016 Marketing Intern, Plasma Inc., Vancouver

Wrote text for flyers, supported team, helped at the events, posted news on Facebook

2015 Crew Person, Talba Ltd., Vancouver

- Greeted customers
- Took orders
- Prepared food
- Ensured that safety regulations are met
- Met target goals during shift
- Responsible for cleanliness
- Ensured that items were well stocked

Extra-curricular activities

Swimming Instructor, Swim Club, Vancouver

Volunteered as Lifeguard

References upon request

Figure 7.5 Sample résumé 5

Poor design and layout. This resume is written in different fonts making it difficult for the reader to quickly grasp the main points.

Inappropriate and missing contact details. Hotmail.com is not an appropriate address that demonstrates your professionalism. No phone number included – make sure that all contact details are provided and double-check that they are correct.

Spelling mistake. Always proof-read your work for typos and grammatical mistakes.

Overused buzz words without explanation. While it can be tempting to include descriptive words that you think recruiters want to read such as "team player" or "good communicator," it is far more important to demonstrate you have the skills and qualities employers are looking for.

Inaccurate information provided. Don't forget to put your degree in resume. In addition, the location of the institution where you earned your degree must be included as well. If your university grades are not strong, better leave them out.

Missing information. Dates of employment are missing.

Avoid using abbreviations which are not commonly known. Recruiters might not be familiar with technical jargon. If you use abbreviations make sure that you write them out clearly the first time they are used.

Don't use prose to outline your experience. Use bullet points instead to ensure that readers can quickly grasp your key skills and achievements.

Check consistency – if you include the country in one subheading you need to do so in all subheadings.

Simple listing of duties. Don't just state your duties. Use action verbs to highlight your achievements and quantify wherever possible. Rather than "Wrote text for flyers": "Carefully drafted text for weekly flyers. Received praise from Deputy Head of Marketing for my compelling writing skills."

Simple listing of duties with too many bullet points. Use maximum five bullet points to highlight your experience and achievements. Instead of "Greeted customers and took orders": "Addressed customer needs appropriately and contributed to improved customer satisfaction ratings" Instead of "Met target goals during shift": "Communicated effectively with team members to meet target goal during shift" Instead of "Ensured that items were well stocked": "Monitored stock resulting in 5% less wastage."

Provide more detail and use action verbs to get across your qualities and skills. Better: "Coached swimmers of different levels on proper techniques," "Organized annual swimming competition," "Established positive relationships with parents and care takers."

Include where and when. Better: "20xx-20xx, Lifeguard, Boat Club, Vancouver." "Monitored swimming pool during summer holidays," "Educated members on water safety and its implications," "Updated safety guideline and created new leaflets for members."

Don't include this statement – employers will ask for references if they are interested. Use valuable space in your resume to include relevant content which is tailored to the job you are applying for.

TIP 7.2 On your résumé, write the name of your educational pro-gramme *exactly* as it appears on your academic transcript.

Language skills and résumés

Often it is hard to know how to convey language skills on a résumé, or if you should even bother noting anything about language skills.

When to state language skills

First, you need to identify whether your language skills are relevant for the company. If the job description indicates a preference for candidates with multilingual capabilities you should definitely include your language skills, including the level of proficiency with the needed language. For example, if you are fluent in Chinese Mandarin and the company you are applying for has Asian clients or facilities in Mandarin-speaking regions then it makes sense that you emphasize your Mandarin skills on your résumé.

If the job description seeks candidates with a specific language make sure that you highlight this specific language skill. If you have a language skill which is not explicitly asked for in the job description, find out whether this language skill is relevant for the company, its customers, or clients. If your language skills are not relevant, it is better to feature other skills that are beneficial for the company.

How to state language skills

Determining your language proficiency is not an easy task. Depending where you are located there may be no universal standard of measurement. Even if standards of measurement are available, recruiters or hiring managers might not be familiar with them. However, it is important to provide evidence of how well you have mastered a language.

The following terms are commonly used in English job descriptions to describe required language proficiency. These terms are understood in all English-speaking countries across the world:

- Native speaker.
- Near native/fluent.
- Excellent command/highly proficient in spoken and written communication.
- Very good command.
- Good command/good working knowledge.
- Basic communication skills/working knowledge.

If you are applying for a job in Europe you could describe your level of language proficiency using the Common European Framework of Reference for Languages (CEFR). This framework provides a clear and easy way for comparing language qualifications. It identifies what you should be able to do in listening, speaking, reading, and writing at each level of language proficiency.

How the CEFR works is illustrated in Table 7.4. Use the table to determine your level of proficiency. A more detailed version of the CEFR is available from www.coe.int/en/web/common-european-framework-reference-languages

Many recruiters outside Europe, and even some within Europe, might not be familiar with the CEFR. We therefore advise you to use the more commonly used descriptions used in English-speaking countries and state the CEFR descriptor in brackets:

Commonly used descriptions for language proficiency	CEFR descriptor
Native speaker	–
Near native/fluent	Proficient user (C2)
Excellent command/highly proficient	Proficient user (C1)
Very good command	Independent user (B2)
Good command/good working knowledge	Independent user (B1)
Basic communication skills/working knowledge	Basic user (A1 to A2)

Proficient User	**C2** Mastery	Can understand with ease virtually everything heard or read. Can express him/herself spontaneously, very fluently and precisely, differentiating finer shades of meaning even in more complex situations.
	C1 Effective Operational Proficiency	Can understand a wide range of demanding, longer texts, and recognize implicit meaning. Can express him/herself fluently and spontaneously without much obvious searching for expressions.
Independent User	**B2** Vantage	Can interact with a degree of fluency and spontaneity that makes regular interaction with native speakers quite possible without strain for either party.
	B1 Threshold	Can understand the main points of clear standard input on familiar matters regularly encountered in work, school, leisure, etc. Can deal with most situations while travelling in areas where the language is spoken.
Basic User	**A2** Waystage	Can understand sentences and frequently used expressions related to areas of most immediate relevance (e.g. very basic personal and family information, shopping, local geography, employment).
	A1 Breakthrough	Can understand and use familiar everyday expressions and very basic phrases aimed at the satisfaction of needs of a concrete type. Can introduce him/herself and others and can ask and answer questions about personal details.

Table 7.4 Common European Framework of Reference for Languages

You can state your language skills either under the "Key skills" section or a separate "Language skills" sections of your résumé. Here's an example of a separate section:

Language skills

German: Native speaker
English: Near native/fluent (Common European Framework of Reference, C2)
Italian: Very good command (Common European Framework of Reference, B2)

Even better, state your language proficiency in these sections but also demonstrate that your language skills will add value to the company. Providing specific examples and highlighting your accomplishments such as:

- Student assistant at Dean's Office: Supported preparation for Chinese delegation visit to our university. Translated Chinese travel and food requirements into English and answered general email questions.
- Volunteered for buddy groups at university: Each semester, helped incoming exchange students from China to settle and find their way around university.

Make sure that you don't exaggerate your language skills. Adhere to the commonly used descriptors or frameworks. Recruiters will quickly identify whether you indeed have the language skills stated in your résumé by asking you questions in this language.

Common questions

In preparing or improving your résumé, you'll likely have questions. We answer the most common ones below.

1. Do I need to include an "objective statement" at the top of my résumé?
No and yes.

If you are applying for a job and are asked to submit both a cover letter and résumé then it is not necessary to include an objective statement in your résumé. If you intend to hand-out your résumé at a networking event, career fair or to people you meet, you should include an objective as otherwise your counterpart will not understand what kind of job you are looking for. Your objective statement should be clear and concise – no longer than two lines, including what type of job you are looking for (i.e. full-time, part-time, internship), the industry, and what skills you would like to use.

Here is an example of a good objective statement:

OBJECTIVE
_____

To obtain an internship position in the automotive industry involving mathematical modelling and data analysis.

2. Should I include a section on "hobbies, sports or personal interests" near the end of my résumé? **No.**
There is no place for these in a professional résumé. Consider this: You might like to include "I love travelling." A potential employer will read this as "She's just going to want extra vacation for her trips. She's not really serious about work."

3. Must I include every job I have had and every educational programme I enrolled in on my résumé? **No.**
You can exclude jobs or education from several years ago. If you are completing your first university degree, then don't have anything in your résumé about high school especially for jobs in North America. That is ancient history and you are a much different person now. You can also exclude jobs you held for just a short time.

4. Can I exaggerate a little to make my accomplishments and past activities seem more impressive on my résumé? **No and yes.**
You cannot mislead or provide inaccurate information on your résumé. Don't make your previous job, or a skill or accomplishment something it was not.

However, you can present yourself in the best possible light. With respect to employment, suppose you worked as a cashier at a local market or grocery store. You can write this in your résumé:

- Provided friendly and patient customer service during peak times

or:

- Scanned products

The first much better reflects the kind of person you are.

With regard to education, suppose in your first year of university studies you did not earn very good grades. On your résumé you can provide your GPA like this:

- GPA in marketing courses: 3.8/4 – GPA in last 20 courses: 3.7/ 4 – Overall GPA – 3.4/4

By doing this, you can quickly show that you have steadily increased your GPA and highlight your strong grades in particular subject areas.

5. Do I need to include references on my résumé, or attach these to my résumé? **No.**
Don't include references because it's assumed you will provide the references either at the interview, or after the interview.

6. Should I pay for someone to write my résumé for me? **No.**
This is something you can and should do yourself. Would you hire someone to write a love song to your sweetheart? Not likely. The same applies to your résumé.

7. Where do I go for help with my résumé?
The first and best place to ask for assistance is the career office at your university. The staff there have many years of experience, as well as resources, to help you write your best possible résumé. However, remember that they will not write it for you.

8. Should "Education" always go after "Key skills," or should I put "Work experience" first?
If you are about to graduate or have recently graduated then "Education" goes first, because what you offer a potential employer

is your education. Only in very rare cases (perhaps someone who studied part-time) should "Work experience" be placed before "Education" for current students or recent graduates.

9. I use an "English" first name, but that is not my official name. How do I deal with this on my résumé?
Place your everyday name in parenthesis like: Xiu Ying (Sally) Zhang.

10. I am non-native English speaker, intending to work in an English-speaking country. Should I state my Test of English as a Foreign Language (TOEFL) or International English Language Testing System (IELTS) score? **It depends.**
If you are writing a résumé for a university application, then the readers of your résumé are most likely familiar with this specific test and the scoring. However, many recruiters (especially native English speakers) won't understand TOEFL scores or those of similar tests. If you are applying for a job where you are required to be fluent in English we would advise you to not to state the TOEFL test on your résumé. Your résumé and cover letter speak for themselves and show the recruiter that you are indeed able to communicate effectively in English.

11. During my job search, I found a really interesting job for which I would like to apply for. However, the job requires working in a language that I am not proficient with. Should I still apply? **No.**
In this case, recruiters are looking for candidates who are able to speak and read the language in which the job advertisement was posted. Applying will be waste of your time, no matter how keen you might be about the position.

All I have is my education

International students sometimes encounter problems writing a résumé because they have limited work experience, especially if they were prevented from working due to the restrictions on student visas, or for other reasons. Or perhaps you had no time or interest in working while being a student.

But "only" having experience as a student is really not a problem. All the skills that employers are looking for are those you demonstrated in your classes:

- communication skills (reading, writing, speaking, listening);
- capacity for learning and problem-solving;
- teamwork, including social skills (ethics, positive, attitude, responsibility); and
- willingness to adapt to changing circumstances and to transfer knowledge to new situations.

You've learned and practised these skills in all your classes and assignments. So, if you have little or no employment experience, expand the "Education" section of your résumé. Here's how, drawing from the résumé earlier in this chapter:

EDUCATION

2017 – Present	**University of British Columbia, Vancouver, Canada**
	Bachelor of Arts, Double Major: Journalism, and Creative Writing; Minor: German

- specializing in twentieth-century American literature, especially short stories;
- wrote an 18 page essay on the influence of women writers in the United States after 1950, titled "Out of the Kitchen!," for a fourth-year course earning a grade of A+ (the professor wrote, "This is a wonderful paper: original and very well researched");
- member of a three student team that designed a website as part of our mandatory fourth-year applied journalism course (the assignment earned a grade of 84 per cent and can be viewed at www.appliedjournalstudent.com);
- gave a 10 minute presentation in German on "The rise and fall of e-books in Germany in the 21st century" for a third-year German class (the professor noted that, "This was among the best presentation to the class, especially the use of images");
- GPA: B average overall; B+ German language courses; A– for fourth-year courses.

Keep in mind that employers are interested in hiring you because you are a student or have very recently been a student!

Cover letter

Once you have mastered writing your résumé, you are probably not too keen on tackling the next hurdle: drafting a cover letter for your application. Actually, there is an ongoing debate whether cover letters are still required as part of applications. Due to the popularity of social profiles and résumé scanning, some companies do not want cover letters while others do so.

Should you therefore bother writing a cover letter? Based on our experience, we recommend that in most cases you should include a cover letter in your application package. Whether a cover letter is needed and the exact format depends in part on where in the world you are applying. What follows assumes that you are applying for jobs in North America and Europe where cover letters are common.

Why a cover letter?

As an international student who might not have much work experience you will find it useful to write a cover letter as you get the chance to highlight your skills and motivation. Cover letters also demonstrate that you are serious about the job application.

However, there are some exceptions such as if you are applying online and there is no place for you to upload or post a cover letter. Furthermore, if the company identifies which documents you should submit and the cover letter is not listed then you don't need to include a cover letter.

As an alternative to a full cover letter you can also send an email cover note if that is possible. Your email should be crafted very well and should include three shortened, tailored paragraphs of your full cover letter. In the subject header of your email you should follow the instructions provided in the job advertisement (such as a reference number). If there are no instructions, use "Application for [job title]" as the subject line. Mention in the email that you attach your résumé and then don't forget to actually attach it (forgetting the attachment is a common mistake).

A well-written cover letter can be the door-opener for an interview – it actually also helps you to prepare for an interview. If there are many candidates applying for the job, the cover letter can play a crucial role. You should therefore spend sufficient time in drafting a cover letter which stands out.

Employers ask for a cover letter because they want to quickly assess whether you are the right candidate for the job they are trying to fill. They expect that you are able to express your interest and motivation in the job and the organization convincingly. They want to find out whether you are able to communicate your strengths, qualifications, and experience in a structured way.

You dramatically enhance your chances of being called for an interview by stating in your cover letter that you have already spoken with a particular person in your desired organization. This will most likely raise the recruiter's interest in you as it shows that you have already done your research about the employer.

Appearance, layout, and style

Similar to your résumé, you need to make sure that the cover letter is easy to read. If the employer doesn't provide specific instructions, then you should limit your cover letter to one page or around 400 words in four to five short and concise paragraphs.

Your cover letter should be laid out like a formal business letter. Your résumé and cover letter should come across as one package, so ensure that you use the same font (minimum size 10 sans-serif font). Your text should be left aligned or justified and your name and address should be at the top, right hand corner of your cover letter.

You should address your cover letter to a specific person (where possible) such as "Dear Ms …" or "Dear Mr …." If a name is not given in the job advertisement, contact the employer and ask whom you should address your cover letter. As a last resort you can use "Dear Sir/Madam" if you don't have a name. End the letter with "Yours sincerely" and your signature.

While you can use bullet points or subheadings in your cover letter to structure it, don't use bullet points in the final document. Aim for a cover letter that comes across as a formal business letter. Unlike in your résumé, you can write the cover letter in the first person, using "I." Use positive language and actions words to show that you're enthusiastic about the job and the organization.

Content

The content of the cover letter usually starts with stating what role you are applying for and where and when you saw the job advertisement. If a reference number was provided make sure that you include this as well. If one of your network members recommended you apply, be sure to mention this.

Then outline why you are interested to work for this specific employer and your motivation to apply for the advertised job. It would be best if you could draw from information provided by previous conversations with employees from this organization (see Chapter 6 on informational interviews). For example, you could state in your cover letter that you have already spoken with a particular person in your desired company. This will most likely raise the recruiter's interest in you as it shows that you have already done your research about the company.

If you did not get the chance to speak with employees beforehand, try to refer to positive information about the employer that you have found on their website or in the news. You can also refer to knowledge that you might have acquired in your studies related to the organization or sector.

You should then briefly outline your current situation and why you are in the job market. Students sometimes make the mistake of assuming that the cover letter is simply a brief version of their résumé in prose. They "cut and paste" parts of their résumé in the cover letter, annoying recruiters and hiring managers as they need to read repeated information.

Don't just repeat information in your résumé as then the cover letter has no value. What makes the cover letter different from the résumé are the details you can provide. These include: when you first heard of the job advertisement, past contacts with people working there, your future plans, and how you will excel at the job.

As with your résumé, your cover letter should be tailored to the organization and position you are applying for. Review the job description and specifications to identify two or three situations where you have shown qualities and skills which the employer is looking for.

You might find it difficult to identify and choose only two or three situations, however, it is important that you stick to only a few examples as otherwise your cover letter is too lengthy and superficial. Highlight and explain your chosen situations and achievements.

You should end your cover letter by emphasizing that you are looking forward to the opportunity to discuss your suitability further at an interview and that you are awaiting a response in due course.

Finally, proof-read your cover letter. Check for correct vocabulary, grammar, spelling, and punctuation. Double-check if the organization's name, name of the recruiter and address are correctly written. Ask one of your friends or colleagues to review your cover letter.

Below, in Table 7.5, is the most common structure of a cover letter. You cannot go wrong by using this for just about any application.

An effective and well written cover letter is shown in Figure 7.6 below. Note how in a little over 300 words the applicant has communicated a significant amount of information. Would you offer this individual an interview? Why?

Speculative cover letter

Only a third or less of job openings are advertised by organizations. This is the so-called "visible" job market. The majority of jobs are not advertised and are on the "hidden" job market. These jobs are not listed on any job site and companies are not promoting these jobs. This might be due to several reasons such as that the company is reducing expenses in advertising.

If you identified a company in your job search process (see Chapter 6) for which you would like to work but you can't find any job advertisement you can reach out to them by inquiring about upcoming opportunities. Similar to the cover letter you would send to advertised job openings, try to find out to whom you need to address your cover letter. Research the company in detail.

Paragraph	Content	Approximate length
Opening	• Where did you see or hear about the job advertisement? • Why are you applying for this specific organization and this specific job? Hint: If applicable, refer to conversations you have had with others in the organization as this will give you an advantage over other candidates by demonstrating a keen interest in the position.	4–7 lines
Introduction	• Why are you looking for a job at this time? What is your current situation? What is your background?	4–5 lines
"Heart" of the cover letter	• Why are you the best candidate for this job? Highlight 2–3 examples of your experiences, skills, competencies and accomplishments which match the job description and specifications outlined in the job advertisement. Hint: Focus on those experiences and skills that are relevant and beneficial for the organization and which set you apart. Perhaps something from your experience as an international student?	~ 11 lines
Closing	• Emphasize that you are looking forward to the opportunity to discuss your suitability further at an interview. • Sign off with "Yours sincerely"	2–3 lines

Table 7.5 Structure of a cover letter

Jane Smith
University Road 1111
Vancouver, Canada, V3X H7
Tel. 123-456-7777
E-mail: janesmith@unimail.ca

Maria Johnson
Recruitment Manager
Amazing Tech Enterprises
14 Bond Street
Vancouver, Canada V1D 2C3

October 12, 2018

Dear Ms. Johnson,

I was excited to see on Jobs.com that your company is searching for a Marketing Coordinator. I am drawn to the opportunity to join Amazing Tech Enterprises because it is a fast-growing and innovative company which fosters professional growth and development for employees. Last month I met with Mario Kolson who graduated from my university two years ago. As a software engineer at Amazing Tech Enterprises he works with a multinational team of developers on various projects. In my discussions with him, he emphasized the entrepreneurial spirit and collaborative culture at Amazing Tech Enterprises which confirmed my interest in your company.

I am currently in my final year of a BA Business Management degree with a special emphasis on marketing at the University of British Columbia. My academic background in the study of marketing combined with my practical marketing experience gained through extra-curricular activities as well as my wide range of relevant transferable skills, have prepared me to make a positive contribution to the success of your company.

As Head of Marketing of the university Entrepreneurship Club, I collaborated with my team to organize several large events. This experience improved my teamwork skills and my ability to work under pressure. As part of my business degree, I created and delivered effective presentations which continuously received grades A and A+.

I have proven my ability to adapt to new situations by having lived and studied in two different countries. Facing several bureaucratic hurdles and dealing with cultural differences helped me to advance my problem-solving skills and my ability to cope with stressful situations.

Your company's forward-thinking environment combined with my academic knowledge and my passion for marketing have prepared me to make a strong and immediate impact at your company.

Thank you for your time and consideration. I look forward to hearing from you soon.

Yours sincerely,

Jane Smith

Figure 7.6 Sample cover letter

Your cover letter should clearly explain why you are applying to the company and outline your motivation. Specify what type of job you are looking for and when you could start. Outline what you can offer the company, instead of what you can gain or want (this is important!). You can use the STAR method to do this (see Chapter 8) to highlight specific examples where you make a direct link between your skills and experience and the requirements of the company. Attach your résumé and wait about one or two weeks and then follow up by emailing or making a phone call.

Waiting

Few things are as frustrating as spending the time and energy to submit a first rate job application and then hear nothing for weeks and weeks. Or perhaps you've received a "Dear Applicant, Thank you for your application" email or text but nothing more. Should you follow up? Is the hiring done? Do you still have a chance for an interview? Has your wonderful application – heaven forbid – been misplaced?

Our advice is to assume that if you are not contacted it is because you will not be offered an interview. That sure sucks, but remember this is a job market with buyers (employers) and sellers (you and other job seekers). To avoid feeling low, have numerous applications on the go at the same time. This way there is no time to dwell on any individual ones.[3]

But then, the most amazing thing happens … you get a call for an interview!

Notes

1   Because résumés are so important and so fiendishly difficult to write well, there are many books and other sources that aim to show you how do to this. If you need more assistance after reading this chapter, try Richard N. Bolles, *What Color is your Parachute? A Practical Manual for Job-Hunters and Career-Changers* (Berkeley, CA: Ten Speed Press). A new edition is published every year.

2 If you're looking for a job in the United States and need more assistance, look at Dan Beaudry, *Power Ties: The International Student's Guide to Finding a Job in the United States* (North Charleston: Independent Publishing Platform, 2014).

3 If you are applying to a lot of positions, you might find the job application tracker called *Huntr* useful (see www.huntr.co). It keeps track of your job search in a Kanban board, with columns for jobs you want to apply to, as well as ones you've applied for. You can also add company data and attachments such as résumés sent, conversations, etc.

Match (II)
The interview

*What lies behind us and what lies before us are tiny matters
compared to what lies within us.*

Ralph Waldo Emerson

Introduction

You landed an interview – congratulations! Your application effort
paid off and you convinced the recruiter that you might be, at least
on paper, the right person for the job. During an interview, the
potential employer wants to assess whether you indeed are suitable as a new employee or intern.

   This chapter prepares you for the interview(s) you will have
to face. And, yes, there will be more than one! After reading
this chapter you will feel more comfortable in interviews and
be prepared to answer any questions you are asked. In fact, this
chapter tells you what the questions are that you will be asked.
Lastly, in the chapter you will learn how to showcase your international education whether the interview is in your host country,
your home country, or another location.

Understanding interviews

Interviewing techniques differ immensely from country to country
but also from organization to organization and even from recruiter

to recruiter. At the end of the day, however, every recruiter and hiring manager wants an honest and well-rounded person who will work effectively and smoothly in a professional manner.

As an international student you might find the prospect of being interviewed even more daunting than the résumé writing. While you had time to carefully select your words and phrases on the résumé and cover letter, you will now be asked to perform on the spot during an interview. Speaking in a language that may not be your native tongue you will be in situations where you are unsure about what to expect. On top of all that, you want to demonstrate that your international studies have given you special skills and knowledge.

Similar to résumé writing you need to prepare for interviews and practice your interviewing skills. While preparing for interviews always ask yourself two questions: "Why should they hire me?" and "How can I add value?"

You are an international student who brings a valuable skill set and experience to any workplace. Studying abroad requires language skills, proactivity, persistence, the ability to interact with diverse individuals, and adaptability to new environments. These are all skills that employers are looking for in candidates. We will help you to highlight these skills later in the chapter.

It is likely that the person interviewing and hiring is under as much stress as you. The manager hiring a new member of a team is doing so because there is too much work for the current team. Very likely the hiring manager hears her boss saying: "When will this work get done? I hope soon!"

Hiring the wrong person will mean the work gets done badly or does not get done at all. Hiring the wrong person will mean weeks or months of procedures to terminate the employment of the new hire. And then having to go through the whole hiring process again. And, most importantly, some pointed questions from their supervisor. If you think being interviewed is stressful, then consider the person on the other side of the table!

Interview expectations

Depending on the culture of the country where you are applying for a position, interviewers expect you to take a more active role or a more passive role.

In most Western countries, the interview is a two-way communication between the recruiter and you, the candidate. Interviewers expect you to be able to expand and elaborate on your answers and to come across self-assured and confident. They expect you to look at them directly when answering questions. In the interview both parties have the chance to find out if there is the right fit. In other words, you are also interviewing the employer!

Furthermore, you are expected to sell yourself during the interview. The interview is a tool to market yourself. Interviewers want to see that you are proactive and self-confident. You are expected to not just state *what* you did during your studies, or in a previous job or internship but to sell it, by showing *how* you made a positive impact in the classroom or workplace. You should never over-sell yourself and exaggerate your achievements, but likewise do not be too modest and hold-back.

Landing interviews can be very difficult if you are a foreigner. I am Taiwanese and studied in Germany, where I looked for a job. I was most successful in being invited for an interview when I called the contact person mentioned in the job advertisement before submitting my application and asked questions about the job. I then mentioned this conversation in the cover letter. This strategy helped me to increase my chances of being offered a phone interview. The more interviews I got, the more practice I had, the better I performed.

If possible, I recommend doing an internship while looking for a job. While an intern, I showed passion about what I was doing and spoke in a very confident manner. While networking – such as inviting colleagues to have coffee and lunch – I learned key words and phrases to showcase my know-how.

Like many cases in life, there will be people who are open to help and people who look down on you just because you are not one of them yet. I asked specific questions of those people who were open. Talk to as many people as possible, sending strong messages to everyone you encounter that you are looking for a position.

Meiyu Huang

It is important that you clarify what *your* achievements were. Recruiters want to know what your individual contribution was in a team or project task. In an interview you should shift your focus from "we" to "I" when discussing team projects or work. This becomes even more relevant in so called behavioural/ scenario- or competency-based interviews. More on this later in the chapter.

Recruiters also expect you to ask relevant and meaningful questions. In fact, some recruiters value the questions you ask the most, as they demonstrate to the recruiter that you did your research and that you are taking the interview process seriously. Questions you might want to ask are: "What are the best/most difficult aspects of working in this organization?", "What do you see as unique about your organization compared with your major competitors?"

In non-Western cultures, your role in the interview may be more passive and modest. Direct eye contact with the recruiter should be minimized, and you are expected to answer questions only when being asked so. The atmosphere might feel to you more like a test rather than a conversation. Likewise, you should only pose questions if you explicitly are allowed to do so.

On-campus services and interviews

Your university probably has a career office or service. You would be wise to visit it and see what it offers in regard to interviews. The career office may even conduct practice or mock interviews for you. In any case, the office will have resources to help you prepare for interviews.

Some employers conduct on-campus interviews that tend to be coordinated by the career office. Signing up for these will encourage you to prepare your résumé and, if offered an interview, to practise your interview skills.

However, preparing for interviews and becoming excellent at them is largely a do-it-yourself project. Your university and programme can give you the tools, but you must wield them yourself to get a job. As a proactive student, you already know this.

Interview types

Interviewers are interested in three key aspects about you:

1. Are you qualified? That is, can you do the job?
2. Are you motivated? Why do you want the job?
3. What is your personality? Do you fit with those already at the workplace?

To discover if you are the right candidate, interviewers have different types of interviews at their disposal.

Below are the eight major interview types along with the typical questions asked in each.

Traditional, face-to-face, one-on-one interview

Just you and one interviewer, the most common type of interview. A traditional interview entails straightforward questions about your experience, background, and personal qualities, such as "Why did you choose to study as an international student?", "How would people who know you describe you in three words?", and "What is your biggest achievement?"

Panel interview

A panel interview is the same as a face-to-face interview but it consists of a panel of several interviewers who are interviewing you at the same time. The panel members are usually employees from different areas of the organization. Taking turns, each of them will ask you questions.

Group interview

Several candidates are invited for an interview. You and the other candidates are asked questions in turn. All candidates introduce themselves, pose questions to other candidates, or get involved in a group discussion on a certain topic. You should not see the other candidates as competitors because employers use this interview type to find out how you work in a team and how you interact with others.

Build rapport with the other candidates, listen, acknowledge their comments, and bring the discussion forward. Be supportive of others in the interview and help them look good. That will get you the job! After all, if you were an employer, isn't that the person you would hire?

Case interview

In the past, mainly consulting firms used case interviews to find out how applicants deal with problems that have no right or wrong answers. For example, applicants were given a business problem such as "How can company xx double its growth?" or a puzzle such as "How many tennis balls fit into a bus?" The intention of these questions was to evaluate applicants' problem-solving and thinking skills.

Nowadays, organizations ranging from start-ups, major international organizations, and NGOs use case questions to identify how applicants approach a problem. The best way to handle a case question or puzzle is to remember that there is no right or wrong answer. What is important is how you approach the question or problem. Use the skills in Chapter 4 to succeed in these interviews, which are much like the tests you've written in your courses.

Often a case interview is incorporated as part of a traditional or group interview. At times you may be given a period of time (20 or 30 minutes) at the start of the interview to answer a case question.

The more you prepare the better. There are many online resources to practise case questions and specific case interview books.[1] Ask classmates to do interview case questions together or participate in case competitions. If you have trouble finding practice partners there are web-based resources that will aid you as you practice this kind of interview.[2]

Sequential interview

In a sequential interview you are interviewed several times by different people of the organization on the same day. Questions get more challenging and in-depth as the day progresses. At the beginning of the day the questions focus on whether you can do the job. Later in the day you have interviews with more senior members of the organization who will assess your motivation and personality.

Telephone interview

You might get asked to participate in an initial phone interview. This call is used as a first screening to see if you have the potential to be invited for a full interview. Recruiters want to find out whether you are truly interested in the job and that there is evidence that you are a good fit for the job. Prepare for telephone interviews the same way as you would for face-to-face interviews.

Schedule the interview for when you can fully focus in a quiet place. Have your application package and job description in front of you, so you can glimpse at them when needed. If you are using a mobile phone ensure that it is charged and that you have good reception. Dress in business casual attire to help put you in an interview mindset; stand up and smile – this will give you more energy and this will transfer to your voice. Listen actively, ask for clarification if needed and speak clearly and slowly when answering.

Videoconferencing interview

Videoconferencing interviews, using Skype, WhatsApp, or other platforms are increasingly popular among employers as they are cost and time efficient. Make sure that all your technical equipment is working before the time of the interview. Check internet connection, lighting, background, and make sure to turn off other programmes running on your computer.

When preparing for a videoconference interview dress as you would for a face-to-face interview. Look directly at the camera, not the screen, to maintain eye contact with the interviewer. Sit upright and remember your body language. Have a background that looks professional (like a bookcase), rather than say a rack of clothing.

Recorded video interviews

Just like videoconference interviews, recorded video interviews are a cost and time efficient way for employers to filter candidates. Normally, you will be asked to book a time slot to record your video. You will be given guidelines on how to prepare for the interview regarding lighting and screen resolution.

In your allocated time slot you will need to answer a set of questions which appear on the screen. Most likely you will be asked a mix of motivational questions and competency/behavioural interview questions (see the next section for further information). You might get the chance to provide additional information at the end of the recording, or reinforce points you've made earlier. Prepare very well for the final minutes as they allow you to differentiate yourself from other candidates.

My experience as an international student from Peru in Germany has been life changing. I have overcome my fears and grown as a person.

Two key factors for eventually being successful in finding a job in a country that is not my home country: my resilience and my willingness to learn the German language.

After submitting my application documents, I eagerly waited to receive a call from the HR department. When I eventually received an invitation for my very first interview I was very happy but also very anxious. I prepared a lot for this interview but unfortunately I wasn't selected. I applied to another company and got invited again, but wasn't selected – again. It was hard to receive these rejections, but I stayed motivated and kept my spirits up. I was grateful to receive the interviewer's feedback, which made me realize which areas I should focus on in order to improve my performance next time.

I only had limited German language skills when I started my interviews. I realized that it was essential for me to improve my language skills to increase my chances and achieve my goal. I took additional language classes and when I got invited to another interview I performed much better and finally I achieved my goal.

Valentina Nahuero

Categories of interview questions

The questions asked during an interview fall into three different categories: technical, strength-based, and behavioural/competency. By understanding these categories, you will better know how to respond.

Technical questions

Interviewers who hire for jobs that require specific technical knowledge will use technical interview question to assess your thought processes and problem-solving skills as well as your specific skills and knowledge. For instance, if you are applying for a position requiring knowledge of financial accounting standards, you may be asked about recent revisions made by the International Accounting Standards Board. Alternatively, if you are being interviewed for a job dealing with international refugees, you might be asked to describe the current work of the UNHCR, the United Nations Refugee Agency.

To prepare to answer technical questions, review material from your courses that relate to the job you are being interviewed for, and the work of the organization. Even if you are not asked specific technical questions, you can sprinkle your technical knowledge as you answer questions throughout the interview.

Strength-based questions

Strength-based questions are common for jobs in large public and private sector organizations. This interview format allows interviewers to identify what you enjoy doing rather than what you can do, unlike behavioural/competency-based interviews (see the next section). The assumption is that if you are enjoying what you do, you will perform very well at it.

Strength-based questions are especially useful in identifying the right candidate from a group of recent university graduates. From talking about what you like (and dislike) the interviewer gains insight into your personality and motivation. Most people feel more at ease and relaxed when being asked to talk about things they enjoy. Therefore, the interview feels more personal and natural.

To succeed in these types of interviews, you should be able to identify your own strengths and how they match the job description for the job you are applying for. Think about how your strengths could be used to the advantage of the organization you're hoping to work for.

Your strengths are things you enjoy doing, pick up quickly, or look forward to. Make a list of your own strengths and think about all areas of your life, including your studies, work experience, volunteering, or extra-curricular activities. Ask yourself: "When am I usually at my best?" and "What motivates me?"

Think about activities you like doing, subjects at school and university you really enjoyed, and also about things you don't like doing and your weaknesses. If you are still struggling to identify your strengths you can use websites such as GraduatesFirst (https://portal.graduatesfirst.com/cp/gfv2/login.aspx) or the Clifton Strengths Finder (www.gallupstrengthscenter.com) to help you.

Here is an example how you could respond to a strength-based question such as "What do enjoy doing?" First, you need to identify the strengths that the job description highlights. Let's assume you are applying for a sales role. The job description states that candidates must be good at building and maintaining working relationships, understanding the needs of the business customers and presenting the product or service in a professional way.

As such, you would be expected to enjoy, and be confident in, communicating with a variety of people and have experience to back this up. In this particular example, you could highlight being an international student, being part of group projects in your classes, a member in the university theatre, or your part-time job.

Some examples of strengths-based questions that you will be asked in an interview:

- What kinds of tasks boost your energy?
- What do you like to do in your spare time?
- Do you think this role will play to your strengths?
- What would your closest friend say are your strengths?
- What tasks are always left on your to-do list?
- Have you ever wanted to quit something?

Interviewers like to identify your weaknesses as well as your strengths. Don't be tempted to give a general statement such as "I am a perfectionist." This answer could make you look disingenuous and unauthentic. Think about a time in the past when you really struggled with something. Maybe you don't like sharing a task with others, or you don't enjoy networking or public speaking.

Ensure that you explain how your strengths compensate for this weakness and what you're doing to overcome it. For example, you could state that your weakness is that you have had a hard time sharing a task with others because you believed that doing it on your own would result in a better outcome. This is why on some occasions you have taken on too many projects which overwhelm you, and which in turn frustrate you. Since you realize you have a difficult time sharing a task with others you are now learning to let go, trust others, and share responsibilities. As a result you have now accomplished great things which you wouldn't have achieved by yourself.

Behavioural/scenario-based or competency-based questions

Interviewers use behavioural/scenario-based or competency-based questions to assess whether you possess the soft skills and competencies of the job description. They want to find out how you approached a problem in the past, assuming that past behaviour predicts future behaviour. If you have taken initiative in your extra-curricular activities or during your volunteering experience, it is more likely that you will show this behaviour in a job or internship. As an international student, you took the initiative to study abroad, and this can be the basis of some of your answers.

For example, interviewers might assess your conflict or problem-solving skills by asking you "Tell me about a time were you overcame a challenge" or "Describe a situation when you and your team members disagreed on ideas. What did you do?"

You can best prepare for these kinds of questions by using the so-called "STAR" approach. STAR stands for "Situation," "Task," "Action," and "Result." This approach helps you to showcase your past experience and accomplishments in a clear and concise way.

- Situation: Describe the context in which you were using Who? What? Where? and When? Your example can be from a work or internship experience, volunteering experience, extra-curricular activity, sports activity, or any other experience. Set the scene in a way that the interviewer can quickly understand the situation you faced. As an international student, you will have no problem remembering situations.
- Task: Explain what problem you faced or what goal you had to reach: What was your role? What was your task/goal?
- Action: Outline what action *you* had to take in order to address the situation. What did you do? Explain how *you* solved the problem, how you reached the goal, or how you completed the task. Specify exactly what your contribution was. It is important that you highlight your role in particular (even when you worked in a team) as the interviewer wants to learn about your problem-solving approach, not that of your team mates or others.
- Result: Describe what changed for the better due to your action. What happened? How did it end? Describe what happened because of your action and how the task ended. Emphasize what you accomplished or learned.

If the interviewer asks you "Tell me about a time you overcame a challenge" you could answer using the STAR approach as follows:

- Situation: Last year, during the summer break from university classes, I worked as a waitress in a restaurant.
- Task: One evening, it was very busy with many customers. Due to other staff members being sick, we were understaffed and customers had to wait for their orders. One customer in particular got very angry about waiting and bitterly complained to me.
- Action: I listened carefully to the customer and made sure that I fully understood the reason for her complaint. She had movie tickets with friends after dinner and did not wish to be late. I apologized for the situation and explained to her that we were short-staffed this evening. I assured her that I would do my very best to serve her in time for her to meet her friends and watch the film. I told her that I love watching films myself, and would feel very bad if she missed seeing the film with her

friends. I offered her extra bread and appetizers, which were available immediately. I also offered her a complimentary beverage, which I was able to do without asking for approval from my manager. I went to the kitchen and convinced the cooks to prioritize my customer's order. I then went back to the customer, apologized again for the delay and told her that her order would arrive shortly. Although she had to eat in a somewhat rushed manner, she left the restaurant in time to make her appointment.

- **Result:** The customer and my manager were satisfied with how I dealt with the situation. The customer returned frequently to the restaurant. I learned from this situation that it is extremely important to be able to communicate openly, calmly, and directly with customers and colleagues and to empathize with everyone involved.

As an international student you probably dealt with a lot of issues. If an interviewer asks you to "Describe a time when you faced a stressful situation. How did you deal with it?" remember to draw on your experience. For example you could say:

- **Situation:** In my first year being an international student I faced problems in adjusting to my new home.
- **Task:** In my "Introduction to Management" class students were assigned to teams to prepare weekly presentations. I was quite confident that I could contribute well to my team and looked forward to our first meeting after class. When I showed up for our meeting my fellow classmates were already well engaged in a discussion on how to proceed with the task. I felt left out and that my ideas and contributions would not be valued.
- **Action:** I proactively approached my fellow classmates, shared my concerns and feelings and asked them in a polite but direct manner why they had started without me. I assumed this was because they did not value my input, but to my surprise, my classmates told me that they were not unhappy with me, but rather that they had started the meeting on time. In my home country, it is perfectly acceptable to arrive late to meetings. Once I realized this difference, I adapted my behaviour and

ensured to always be on time for our meetings using tools such as Google Calendar and colour coding specific meetings and events.
- **Result:** My classmates appreciated my efforts and we formed a great team which successfully prepared and delivered weekly presentations. Based on this experience, I learned a lot about cultural differences regarding time management. This experience also improved my teamwork skills as I realized that it is important to proactively address issues in a team and to communicate openly and honestly.

Here is another example of how you could use your international study experience to your advantage in answering behavioural interview questions:

- **Situation:** I spent my third year on a study abroad programme in a country I had always wanted to visit. Initially I was so thrilled to be selected to spend one year abroad. I saw this as a unique opportunity to hone my language skills, to be exposed to a different culture and to grow as a person.
- **Task:** After the first weeks of settling in, the initial excitement of being in a new country had worn off. I started to feel homesick and missed my friends and family. I had made no friends and became frustrated and sad, staying in my student accommodation for most of the time except for classes.
- **Action:** Eventually, I realized that just wishing for a change would not solve the problem. So I decided to take my future in my own hands and looked out for opportunities to meet with people and get active. Back in my home country, I really enjoyed being in the drama club at my school. I therefore tried to find out whether my host university also had such a club. After one of my classes I saw a poster in the hallway which advertised the next theatre club performance. On the day of the performance I approached one of the actors and asked whether they would be looking for new members. The club was indeed recruiting new members and as such I was invited to attend the weekly rehearsal. I made sure to be on time for this meeting and received a very warm welcome from all club members.

- **Result:** Joining the theatre club at my host university was the best decision I could have made. I not only found new friends – local and international students alike – but also improved my language skills by speaking in front of a theatre audience. Through this experience I improved my problem-solving skills by learning how to be proactive and gained more self-awareness.

You should prepare several such stories which demonstrate the relevant skills the company is looking for. At university, for example, you could think about your involvement in team or group work. Maybe there has been a time when your team members and you argued over the next steps in the project – what role did you take and how did you deal with the problem?

Likewise, think about your sport activities – was there a time when you performed really well? How did you meet your goal? Overall, think about any experience where you exceeded expectations, dealt extremely well with a problem, created something new, made things easier, or saved or made money. This does not have to be in a workplace, but can just as well be in the classroom.

Typical interview questions

The number of interview questions is not infinite. In fact, there is a relatively small number of questions that you will encounter in any interview. Below we list all the questions that interviewers are likely to ask.

Opening/warm-up
- Tell me about yourself.
- Talk me through your résumé.
- Why did you apply for this job?
- Why do you want to work here?

Education
- Where did you study? Why did you choose that place?
- What did you study and why did you choose to study this?
- Do you think that your academic programme prepared you well for the real world?

Work experience
- Why did you decide to do an internship or work at company xx?
- What was most rewarding? What was most challenging?
- What was your key learning during this internship/work?

Conflict/problem-solving
- Tell me about a time when there was conflict at work and how you handled it.
- Describe a situation where you were responsible for a task and had problems completing it.
- Tell me about a time when a classmate/colleague criticized your work publicly. How did you react?

Decision-making
- Tell me about a time when you had too many tasks to complete and had to prioritize.
- Describe a situation where you had to make an unpopular decision.
- Describe a time when you faced a stressful situation. How did you deal with it?

Teamwork
- Describe a time when you and your team members argued or disagreed on ideas. What did you do?
- Describe a time when you helped someone in your team.
- Thinking about your last teamwork – what role did you take and why?

Leadership
- Tell me about a time when you had to take charge of a situation that lacked leadership.
- Describe a situation where you have motivated others to follow your lead.
- For what kind of manager do you prefer to work for? Why?

Organization/job knowledge
- What do you know about our organization?

- Who are our main competitors or similar organizations? What are future trends affecting our organization?
- What do you think is the most challenging aspect of the job you are applying for?

Goals/motivation
- What are your short- and long-term goals?
- What is your biggest achievement and why?
- How do you think you can add value to our company?

Self-reflection
- What are your strengths?
- What are your weaknesses?
- How would people who know you describe you in three words?
- What characteristics or qualities do you value most in people?

Closing
- Do you have any questions?
- Why should we hire you? Describe three of your skills that would benefit our company.
- What distinguishes you from other candidates?

You will not be asked all these questions in an interview. However, you can be sure that the questions you will be asked are in the list.

Below we explain how to approach the ten most likely questions that you will have to answer in just about any interview you will ever have.

Decoding common interview questions

As with writing exams, the key to a successful interview is to understand the questions. Below, we decode the ten questions you are most likely to be asked during an interview and demonstrate how to respond. As you will learn, what at first glance looks to be the question is not!

If you are prepared to answer these ten questions, you will have no problem getting an A on any interview.

Tell us about yourself.

Translation: Here's some rope. Want to hang yourself?

Explanation: People who ask this question are looking for potential problems that you might bring with you. They are also curious about your self-image. What do you think about you?

Solution: Your task here is to suggest that you are a reliable person with a good scholarly record who has profited from being in university as an international student, not to blurt out your life. You can answer this question constructively by quoting some positive comments from your professors, references, or past employers.

Duration: Two minutes tops. This is not the place in the interview to go into details.

Why did you apply for this job?

Variation: What kind of work are you looking for?

Translation: Show us how you fit our precise needs.

Explanation: The question asks you to demonstrate what you think the job is about. If your description doesn't match theirs, you can be eliminated.

Solution: If you know exactly what the position entails for (due to the research you've done), then this is easy to answer. If you don't know much about the job, then you're in trouble. The best you can do is turn the question around and ask for more details about the job itself. Say something like, "I'd love to talk about my suitability for the position, but perhaps you could give me some more information about what it specifically involves."

Duration: Up to ten minutes.

What experience/expertise do you have in this line of work?

Variation: What makes you think you'd be good at this job?

Translation: You don't seem to have much experience. You probably can't do this job.

Explanation: Candidates who are entering the professional marketplace and don't yet have the experience that many employers will be asked this question.

Solution: Don't apologize for your lack of experience or say that you're willing to learn. That just makes you look needy. Demonstrate that you have transferable skills from your education, such as research, being able to learn quickly, communication skills, teamwork, and more. Finally, remind the interviewers that you've mastered many things in the past, including succeeding in your international studies, and will do so in the future.

Duration: Up to ten minutes. This is where you sell yourself.

Can you describe an example of how you handled a difficult situation involving other people?

Variation: How did you get along with previous employers, co-workers, or classmates?

Translation: Are you difficult to get along with?

Explanation: All employment positions require strong collaboration and teamwork skills. Hiring someone who can work with others is far better than engaging a brilliant individual who is hard to get along with, especially for entry-level jobs. If interviewers suspect that you might be difficult, you will not be hired. Interviewers look for a tendency to criticize employers or fellow workers. Interviewers may push you into discussing a serious conflict you had with a past employer, co-worker, roommate, or teacher.

Solution: Describe a school or employment situation in which you acted maturely to get people on your side or to defuse conflict. Always emphasize the strong qualities that you demonstrated in resolving clashes and the positives that you took from difficult people and situations. If you're asked for details, don't hesitate to provide them. Find ways of saying nice things about the people who were involved. Never trash talk even the most irritating individuals or their actions. This will simply make you look bad. Your purpose in the interview is to show that you are above any pettiness, even if you've clearly been wronged.

Duration: This can take anywhere from ten to fifteen minutes, depending on the depth of probing.

Can you explain the gap in your work–school history?

Variations: Why did you take a year out between high school and university? Why did it take you five years to complete a four-year programme? What did you do during the year that isn't mentioned in your résumé?

Translation: Are you a quitter, a failure, a slacker?

Explanation: Gaps on a résumé will raise this question as potential employers are curious about what you did during that time period.

Solution: Your task is to show that you are dedicated to school and work. You took time to prepare for international studies, or to prepare or renew your skills. You used the gap time to become a better person, student, and a better employee. Assure the interviewers that you have a serious commitment to the job.

Duration: Five minutes.

Tell us why you became an international student?

Variation: What have you gained for your international education? Why are you planning to obtain employment in this country/city?

Translation: Show how your international studies will help you in this employment position.

Explanation: This is a positive question to better understand you and why you became an international student. The key here is to give a succinct answer. Try to relate your answer to the organization or employment position. For example, don't answer with "I became an international student because my friend did." Rather state, "I became an international student because I had an intense interest in twentieth-century American theater, and the best place to learn more was here." Then, show that being an international student has given you skills such as quickly adjusting to a new environment, interacting with a range of people, and being a proactive individual. Aim to indicate that your international studies are part of a plan that logically took you right to the interview today.

Duration: Up to five minutes.

What is your greatest weakness?

Variation: What personal qualities do you feel you need to work on to be a better person or employee?

Translation: Tell us what's wrong with you so that we can reject you immediately.

Explanation: This question usually comes near the end, when you are getting a bit tired or cocky. It's a serious trap and its purpose is solely to eliminate you as a candidate. It's the question from hell – unless you're prepared for it. Honest but inexperienced candidates are often lured in by this question, especially if they feel that the interview has gone well and that they have a good feeling about the interviewer.

Solution: In fielding this question, provide a weakness that also counts as a strength. Saying something like, "I have a tendency to work a little too hard when I'm completing an interesting project" never lost anyone a job. See also strength-based interviews earlier in this chapter.

Duration: Five minutes tops.

Where do you expect to be in your career in five years from now?

Variation: How do you want your career to develop?

Translation: Are you just looking for a job, or do you want a meaningful career?

Explanation: Employers want to know whether you are a good investment. Will you grow with the organization and into successively responsible positions?

Solution: Show that you are reasonably ambitious, which means doing research on your career and its probable trajectory. You want to convey that you thrive on challenges and opportunities but without giving the impression that you'll set the office on fire. You want to look like someone who will grow and develop in your career, and not quit in three months.

Duration: Up to five minutes.

What are your salary expectations?

Translation: Can we afford you?

Explanation: Your potential cost is always on the employer's mind during the interview, especially if you are an impressive candidate with specialized degrees and experience. Although interviewers know that asking about salary is unprofessional at this stage, they often fish for the information anyway because it helps them decide between equally good candidates. Also, they know that you'll be in a much better bargaining position once they've offered you the job. If you fall into the trap of agreeing to salary now rather than waiting until you're presented with a contract, you'll make their lives easier.

Solution: You never know what kind of pressure you'll encounter during an interview. For this reason, it's a good idea to have a salary range in mind that is based on averages for your profession. But it is important not to negotiate salary unless your hand is forced. Simply explain that you cannot discuss it unless a formal offer of employment has been made and you are seriously considering it. Right now, you'd prefer to concentrate on the issue at hand, which is discovering whether your skills match their needs. Upon being offered the job, you'll enter into the salary negotiation and will be able to leverage the highest possible compensation at that time. Once they make their choice, they won't want to start interviewing again. Be prepared to be reasonable, but also remember that getting higher pay is much easier when you are hired than after you are in place.

Duration: Under normal conditions, this question should be dealt with in less than a minute, since you do not want to commit at this time.

Do you have any questions for us?

Variation: Is there anything that you'd like to ask us?

Translation: This is your opportunity to size us up.

Explanation: A skillful candidate will have compiled a list of questions before the interview and will ask them where appropriate. The rule of thumb for a good interview is that interviewer and interviewee each talk for 50 per cent of the time. This is a clear sign of matchmaking, where two individuals are feeling each other out and engaging in a courtship ritual. Depending on the nature of the interview, this may not be possible. If many people need to be interviewed, or if there is more than one interviewer, your questions may be left to the end of the session. Even if the interviewers are not particularly interested in your questions, they will expect you to have some. Failing to ask questions implies either neediness, lack of interest, or insufficient research on the position and the organization.

Solution: Show that you've done your homework by asking about the job or the organization. Highlighting an issue or problem that it, the industry, or the profession is facing and then seeking your interviewers' opinion is always very effective. Make the most of this opportunity to show off your knowledge and interest. Your questions should not be focused on yourself. It's fine to ask for clarification of some aspects of the position or to elaborate on an earlier answer, but demonstrating your interest in them rather than your needs or desires is most effective here. This approach works well in dating and in job hunting!

Duration: Variable, but prepare a good ten minutes of questions, even if the responses are abbreviated. Here are eight questions to ask at the formal interview:

- Can you describe a typical day on the job?
- What are your organization's three top goals for the coming year?
- What are the biggest challenges in this position?
- What are the major challenges facing your organization?

- What are the career opportunities for someone who excels in this position?
- What is your organization's management style or philosophy?
- What kinds of people succeed best in this organization?
- What kinds of people have not succeeded in this organization?

Responding to difficult question and situations

Interviews are stressful, even for senior executives who have had many of these during their careers. Interviews don't always go the way you imagine they should. Here's how to respond when things go wrong, or when faced with demanding questions or a complex situation.

1. *"On the way home from my interview I realized I screwed up an answer. Can I call or write back to explain?"* **No!**
Once the interview is over, it is over. Interviewers do not want to receive more information or explanations after the interview. This is unprofessional and ensures you are not hired.

2. *"At the end of the interview I felt like I was being pushed out. The last minute of the interview was so hurried. Did I do something wrong?"* **No.**
The interviewers have other things to do. Don't engage in small talk. Once the interview is over, shake hands (if appropriate for the culture of the country), say "Good bye," and quickly leave the room.

3. *"I was asked questions that made me feel uncomfortable, such about marriage and having children. How should I have replied?"*
In many countries it is illegal, or at least unprofessional, to ask personal questions (that is, questions unrelated to the employment position). However, it is surprisingly common for these kinds of questions to be asked in interviews, or in small talk at the end of an interview. In other countries, it is entirely acceptable for questions about age, family, and future plans to be part of interviews.

You might not have to answer these questions as they are considered discriminatory in some countries or you simply do not want to answer these kind of questions. However, you need to make sure that you don't come across combative and aggressive as this could diminish your chances of landing the job. Try to stay calm and diplomatic and use one the following strategies if the interviewer asks you whether you are married and have children.

First, you could rephrase the question and say "I'm not sure I fully understood the question. I suppose you are asking whether I am committed to the job, able to travel, and work late nights. I can assure you that I have a very strong work ethic and am confident I can meet the requirements of this position."

Second, and a little bit firmer is: "I'm not sure I understood the question and in particular how it relates to the job that I'm being interviewed for?" This puts the ball back into the interviewer's court. Most times the question will be dropped, or if asked again will be rephrased and easier to answer.

A third reply is, "I keep business and personal matters separate. I can assure you that my personal life does not affect my ability to excel at this position." This makes clear that you do not wish to make further comments on the topic.

4. "I am a person with a disability. Should I disclose this during the interview?" **It depends.**
If the disability will not impact on your performance at work, there is no need to discuss it during the interview. If the disability could or will have an impact on your performance at work then discuss it. Briefly explain the exact nature of the disability and what, if anything, the employer may need to do to accommodate you in performing your job. Be sure to stress that you can do all the tasks required for the position.

5. "I have an accent. Will that mean that I will not be hired?"
Employers hire because of the contributions a new employee will make. In the interview you will be evaluated as a complete package. Don't apologize for, or try to explain, your accent or any other characteristic over which you have no control.

6. "I have travel plans a couple of months from now. Should I mention these in the interview?" **No.**

Do not bring up future plans during the interview. Should you be offered the position, you can then – and only then – mention travel/vacation plans.

7. "I am thinking that I may return to school or return home in a year. Should I mention this in the interview?" **No.**

Unless you are certain that you will be doing this, you should not mention it. However, you should also be honest with yourself and the potential employer. If you are sure that you will only be able to hold the position for a year, then this is something you should mention during the interview.

> **TIP 8.1** "The interviewers were so nice to me. I'm sure I got the job." Interviewers are nice to everyone interviewed. You are unable to know the outcome of an interview from how the interviewers behave.

Interview preparation

Careful interview preparation takes time and effort. Here are tips on what you should do before the interview and at the interview. The next section shows you what to do after the interview. In many ways the interview is like an oral presentation (see Chapter 5).

Before the interview

- Make sure that you know the location, time, and likely duration of your interview. When you are invited for an interview this information is normally provided. If you don't receive this information write an email or call the employer to ask for this information. You can use this opportunity to also ask whether you need to prepare anything else in advance, what the interview format will be and if there will be case questions.
- Prepare to bring a photo ID in case this is required to enter the building. Plan to bring a professional-looking notebook, folder,

etc. with blank paper, a pen or pencil, your prepared questions, and at least two copies of your résumé.

- Identify how long it will take you to get to the location of the interview, always allocate additional time as you might experience delays.
- Review your application package, including your résumé and cover letter. Read through the job description and look at it against your application. Think about specific examples in your past which match the skills and competencies outlined in the job description (see the STAR approach earlier in this chapter). Remember to also review your strengths to ensure that you are prepared for strength-based questions.
- Prepare your list of references to bring with you on the day of the interview (see the next section of this chapter).
- Learn about the job you are applying for. Review the job description and think about how the job you are applying for fits into the wider company structure. Search on professional networking sites such as LinkedIn for profiles of people with a similar role.
- Do research on the person or people interviewing you. This might help you to establish rapport with them. Search the internet or professional networking sites to find background information such as their role in the company, university attended, international experience, etc.
- Familiarize yourself with the organization. Explore the company website and annual reports. Search for major news about the company using a Google news search and check their social media channels. Consider setting up informational interviews (see Chapter 6) with staff members who aren't on the hiring committee. Try to identify and connect with alumni working at the company (again, see Chapter 6).
- Practice, practice, practice: Do practice runs by speaking out loud in front of a mirror. You can also use software tools such as Big Interview. These tools simulate a real interview. They ask you general or industry-specific questions, record your answers to enable you to send your interview to friends, family, alumni, mentors, or anyone else who could give you valuable feedback. Ask them to focus on: the content and structure of your answers (i.e., coherent answers which are easy to understand and follow

without rambling and too much detail); and your presentation skills (pace, voice quality and tone, energy, posture, eye contact, and hand gestures).[3]

My main goal for studying abroad as an international student for the MBA degree was to shift geographies and industries.

My strategy from the very beginning was to identify previously acquired skills that could be "sold" to an interviewer as cross-functional. This was a long-drawn process since skills had to be tailored not just to job positions, but also to the respective company culture. The career centre at my university remained a constant guiding factor in this process.

Amid all of this, I had the opportunity to work on student-led entrepreneurship initiative which introduced me to a rich network of people on the startup scene. Networking, in my opinion, was the key to my success in the job search process. Through various conversations and guest speeches, I had learned one thing – "never sell yourself short" – and that became my ideology during interviews.

I learned that employers in Germany, unlike in my home country, India, were interested more in "what I could do" instead of "what I had done before" and that gave me the opportunity to better market myself.

After my first interview, I realized that I was rusty on personality questions. To correct this, I practised by sourcing more than 100 questions from the internet and writing short, succinct answers. I still had to differentiate myself from the other non-local candidates. So, I did some of the interviews in German to prove my willingness to integrate into the local environment. And it worked!

Sayalee Shende

References

You may be asked to supply a list of references at the interview. Or you may need to provide references once the interview is complete and you are one of the remaining candidates being seriously considered. In either case, be prepared have your list of references ready and bring it to the interview in case the hiring process is moving quickly, which does happen at times.

Employers ask for references because they want to learn more about you from reliable and objective third parties, such as your professors, supervisors, or co-workers. You will have to choose wisely whom you ask for a reference as these individuals will have to speak favourably about you and provide evidence that you are the right candidate for the job.

Select three references, preferably persons who know something about the type of jobs you are applying for. Of course, it is even better if you can identify someone who works in the organization or sector. However, as an international student you most likely don't have an extensive network yet and you need to think of alternatives.

Your best choice is to ask your professors. This is because professors are seen to be objective by employers and providing references is part of the job descriptions of instructors. Furthermore, professors have a record of your performance, including test scores, class attendance, and performance on other assignments.

Ideally you have others beyond professors whom you can ask to be references for employment applications. Choose people who can evaluate your work performance and your character – if you had a part-time job while studying ask your supervisor or colleagues. Think about your extra-curricular activities. If you worked as a volunteer or got involved in a student or sports club you can ask those who worked closely with you for a reference. Try to avoid including any family members in your reference list. Employers want to learn more about you from unbiased and objective sources.

You always need to ask for permission from your references to forward their name and contact details to your prospective employer. By doing so you can also check whether their contact details are still correct. If you want a glowing reference, you must provide them with a copy of your résumé, the job description of the position you are applying for, and some suggestions about your work experience, skill set, and personality which they should highlight.

Let your references know well in advance that you included them as a reference so that a call or email from your prospective employer does not catch them by surprise. Thank your references for their support and follow-up with them once you learned about the outcome of your job application. Review the material in Chapter 2 on how to ensure your references are the strongest possible.

When preparing your reference list you should adhere to similar principles we have outlined in earlier sections on résumés and cover letters. Make sure that your reference list is clear, concise, and consistent with the same font and format used in your application, check that there are no grammatical or spelling mistakes.

Your reference list should be on a separate page with your name as the heading, followed by your references in order of importance (from most important and relevant to least important). See the sample below.

JAMIE VAN VUUREN

University Road 1111, Vancouver, Canada, V3X 5H7 jvanvuuren@unimail.com, (123) 456–7777 LinkedIn.com/in/jamievanvuuren

REFERENCE LIST

Dr. Samantha Sample
Professor
Marketing and Behavioural Science Division, University of British Columbia
22 Survey Street, Vancouver, A2B C3D
(123) 456 2789, sam.sample@unimail.com

Mr. Jon Dolan
Senior Marketing Manager
Marketing Global, Inc.
1001 Angel Road, Los Angeles, 11111, USA
(654) 372 1544, jon.doe@marketingglobal.com

Ms. Janet Lee
Director
Office of Student Clubs, University of British Columbia
157 Survey Street Vancouver, B2B C7D
(123) 757-4401, janet.lee@unimail.com

On the day of the interview

- Dress appropriately which means anticipating how people are dressed in the company you are applying for. The standard of what to dress for an interview varies from industry to industry. Business attire is suit and tie (men) and skirt or suit (women). Choose neutral colours, shoes that complement your clothes, minimal jewellery, and natural makeup. You should also have well-groomed hair and facial hair, limited or no perfume, clean hands (no chipped nail polish), and no body odour. It is fine to be more formally dressed than those interviewing you.
- Turn off your phone and put it away. Do not display it during the interview.
- Arrive around 5–10 minutes early to settle-in and relax before the interview. Remember to be friendly and courteous with everyone you meet. First impressions matter a great deal.
- Greet the interviewer(s). Write down names when introduced at the beginning so you can respond with their names later.
- Be aware of your body language. Maintain eye contact, sit upright, and act positive and enthusiastic.
- Listen carefully to each question. If you don't understand a question don't be afraid to ask for clarification or re-phrasing. Use the STAR method for behavioural questions. Speak clearly, concisely, and at a steady pace.
- Take brief notes, especially when questions are being asked. These will help you to formulate replies.
- If asked about your background, provide a brief cultural context to your education or work history as necessary. Interviewers may not be familiar with your country's culture.
- Don't ask about salary or benefits as these matters are normally discussed once you have received the job offer.

Immediately after the interview

You may think that once you step out of the interview room, the interview process is over. But that is not the case. There are two tasks still to complete.

First, write down some notes about what went well, what you could improve, etc., to help you plan for future interviews. What questions could have been answered better?

Second, send an email, text, or paper note to the interviewers thanking them for the interview and saying how much you enjoyed meeting them, and confirming your interest in the job. Do this right after the interview (on the same day).

Sending an email or note after the interview demonstrates that you are serious about the position. It also demonstrates the kind of professional individual that you are.

A thank you message should never be more than two or three short paragraphs. What you write is not particularly important; what will be remembered is that you took the time to write and send it.

Here's a sample:

Dear Mr Morris,

It was a pleasure to meet you yesterday and learn more about the Children's Wish Foundation. I appreciate the time you spent reviewing the responsibilities of the outreach coordinator position.

During the interview, you stressed the outreach coordinator's important role of training volunteers. You may be assured that my educational programme in non-profit management, and my previous employment position at the Lakeview Foundation, have prepared me for the coordinator position.

Thank you once again for your time and consideration.

Sincerely,

[your name]

▌The second and third interviews

That many employers are using second and third interviews is a sign of just how seriously organizations take finding the right candidate. It used to be that one interview was enough. These days, however, even three interviews are sometimes seen as insufficient, and hopeful candidates may find themselves going through a roller-coaster ride of sessions that takes many weeks.

This provides some very good reasons for relaxing about the interview process. There's no point in getting worked up about a position that involves several interviews with various people. It's not healthy. Plus, the gap between the first and third interviews gives you time to reflect on the nature of the organization and whether it's right for you.

Interviews at small organizations

Much of what we wrote so far in this chapter applies to interviews at large organizations where there are trained human resources staff. However, many new jobs are with small companies or enterprises. Alternatively you may be interviewed by a professor for a job on campus, perhaps as a research assistant. In these cases, the interviewer probably won't have been trained in interviewing.

Here's what you need to remember for interviews by the owner of a small company or by a manager in a small enterprise:

- He or she is probably just as nervous as you are.
- You have the responsibility to ensure that the right questions are asked.
- It is critical that you put the interviewer at ease with you.
- Following-up after the interview is essential, since the interviewer probably will have a hard time making a decision.
- Try to add the employer to your network. There's a possibility that she or he may hire the wrong person and may be looking for someone in the future.

In many respects, small companies are the ideal environments for personal growth because they tend to be less bureaucratic and provide many more opportunities to develop your professional skills.

The smaller companies cannot invest as heavily in recruitment and must, therefore rely more on networking to find employees. They are also much more likely to accept non-traditional working relationships or take a risk on a new employee who does not fit the typical mould, such as an international student.

For people who are just starting out, innovative small enterprises may be the best places to break in and obtain professional experience.

Hearing back after the interview

The wait after an interview can be lengthy and feel even lengthier. At this point, there's not much you can do, other than continue your job hunt and go to interviews.

Experienced job hunters never put all their eggs in one basket. Instead, they apply for several jobs at the same time. That way, if they don't land one of them, they can focus their energy to other opportunities rather than brooding about the one that got away.

In the labour market, as in any market – whether it involves stocks or oil – there must be a match between the seller (you) and the buyer (the employer). This will not occur immediately and probably not during your first attempt. Wait for a good match between the employment position and your interests and abilities.

But then at last, after just a few days or perhaps many weeks, you receive a phone call or email. Usually a phone call is good news; while an email or text is not. If you are seriously being considered you may be asked to provide your references, if you have not already done so. Or you may be asked for further information.

If you are offered the job, respond promptly, stating that you are considering the job and will get back with an answer in the allocated time. If you are not offered the job ask for feedback to ensure that you can improve for your next interview.

Be aware that some employers try to keep candidates on the hook while they make a decision or negotiate with another job applicant. It's natural for them to look after their own interest, but it's equally important for you to look after yours. If they ask, as they often do, you can tell them that you are interviewing for other comparable positions. If they are reasonable, they will understand. If they are interested in you, this information may prompt them to act more quickly.

■ At last!

After what seems like an eternity, you've signed on the dotted line. You've been hired and know when your first day at your new job will be. Fantastic!

Go and celebrate! Try to remember your first day as an international student, or the first time you even considered studying abroad. Surely, it has been a wonderful journey, with its ups and downs. But you've made it.

Before you start work you might consider sending a short note to those who have helped you along the way: your references, key persons in your network, professors who've influenced you, friends, and family. Then enjoy the feeling of having a job, without yet having to go to work!

■ Notes

1   See, in particular, Marc P. Cosentino, *Case in Point: Complete Case Interview Preparation* (Santa Barbara, CA: Burgee Press, 10th edition 2018).
2   You can try www.preplounge.com/en. Although this site is aimed at those seeking employment with consulting firms, the case interview skills are transferable to all interviews with this type of format.
3   A great book which explains what techniques you can use to adjust your body language, behaviour, and mind-set in a way to overcome your fear in challenging situations such as job interviews is Amy J. C. Cuddy, *Presence: Bringing your Boldest Self to your Biggest Challenges* (New York: Little, Brown and Company, 2015).

Lasting achievements

Though no one can go back and make a brand-new start, anyone can
start from now and make a brand-new ending.

Carl Bard

Introduction

Your first job after completing your education is the start of a new phase of your life. As we explain below, this phase may well include additional education, looking for a job again, and other transitions. Like any transition, the path from school to work will not always be trouble-free.

In this chapter we warn you of pitfalls and show you ways to avoid them, and advise you on how to manage when things don't go well. The chapter is not a long one, since as an international student, you've already developed the skills and aptitude to flourish in your environment, and make your dreams come true.

> Nearly 20 years ago I moved from Hong Kong to Canada as an international student. My years studying abroad changed my life.
>
> My academic performance improved dramatically in the new environment. Far away from Hong Kong – where people walk fast, eat fast, and speak fast – I found quiet spaces to read and learn. Without my close friends around, I relied on my own resources and

was able to blossom. Of course, I experienced tremendous culture shock, but I chose to appreciate and celebrate the differences I encountered.

The skills I acquired in Canada – academic, social, language, and more – helped me to work for global companies: KLM, Cathay Pacific, and Virgin Atlantic. More recently these same skills allowed me to land jobs in English-language schools in Hong Kong.

My years as an international student opened my eyes to see the world anew. Nearly each day since returning home, I have recalled some aspect of my time abroad to remind me that regardless of race and language we all can make our world a better place.

Grace Yau

Your first job

For the first few weeks or months, you may feel much as you did during the start of your international studies. This will be a time of transition and new expectations. Virtually everything will be unfamiliar, and you'll need to figure it out quickly. Fortunately, you've been through this kind of transition before and are well prepared to absorb lots of information and make sense of it.

At first, you may be disappointed by your job. It may have sounded exciting in the interview, but as you settle into it, you begin to realize that you are starting at the bottom. Your customers, students, clients, shifts, projects, and assignments are the dregs, allocated to you because no one else wanted them.

And that's no accident. You were hired specifically because no one was available or willing to do these less appealing tasks. But now that you've got your foot in the door, it's time to demonstrate that you can learn rapidly and contribute, while graciously accepting that you're the new kid on the block.

During your first job, your colleagues and superiors will be assessing your personality more intensively than at any future point in your career. By showing that you are a contributor rather than a whiner at this difficult time, you can leave a powerful impression on them, one that will serve you well when opportunities arise for advancement.

New employees often desire to move ahead quickly. If you think that after two weeks on the job, you've discovered a great new way of doing things that has never been considered before, think again. It's highly unlikely that you'll solve a long-standing problem in such a short time.

At the same time, don't discount your observations either. By being new – and bringing to bear your university knowledge and expertise – you do have a contribution to make. In fact, your newness is a real advantage because it allows you to look at patterns and processes with fresh eyes.

If you want to make a positive contribution – particularly by thinking critically, or outside the box – it is crucial that you strive to maintain that sense of newness, curiosity, and questioning as long as possible. When you combine it with a bit more experience, you will add value to any organization.

Employers frequently complain that many university graduates lack collaborative skills. Therefore, demonstrating that you are a team player from the very first day of work will make a good impression. If you learned how to work in groups at university, this will pay dividends now.

If you are a team player, you may want to immediately be included in projects. The danger here is looking too pushy and aggressive. Be patient. Your superiors and colleagues will feel you out as a person and assess your talents before including you. Don't worry; they'll discover your potential soon enough! When this happens, you may find yourself besieged by requests for assistance.

Trust yourself to make the necessary adjustments. Aim for competence and even excellence, but not perfection. Nobody's perfect, but many people have burned themselves out by trying to be!

As you learn on the job, use the skills that you developed at university. Create a schedule, just as you did at school. Prioritize your tasks, and provide something extra via your research or the way in which you complete projects. Above all, show initiative and take criticism well. Much of your success at work depends on how effectively you used your university time to learn, and hone, your skills.

Instead of being a stressful adjustment, your first weeks or months on the job might just be fun filled and exciting. Hey, you're making money. Unlike in school, you may have your weekends free. And school assignments are a thing of the past. As well, you're meeting new people and learning new skills and abilities.

I never imagined that studying and working abroad – something I wanted so much – was going to be the most ambitious and hardest thing to do in my life. It took me nearly three years to find the right MBA programme, meeting the requirements, and building my resources.

What I didn't realize is that the perfect programme for me would be in Germany. I was not only moving to a new country but moving to an entirely new continent, alone. I knew that I would encounter challenges during my studies that would be amplified by being unaccustomed to the culture and language of a new environment. However, it felt destined as all the pieces immediately fell into place.

I've never regretted my decision to earn my MBA in Europe. Personally and professionally, I have met amazing people, I gained a significant boost to my career, and I found a job beyond my expectations that provides professional development and growth opportunities, and a considerable return on my investment on my MBA.

I have to admit, one of the hardest things about moving to Germany, was leaving behind Ecuador and all that it encompasses: my family, friends, and a good job. Many days I feel homesick, but I am grateful to say my family has supported me every step of the way. My current professional opportunities are incomparable and the satisfaction of conquering the challenges I have faced make it all worth it.

Nadia Alarcon

After the excitement wears off

Occasionally, a sense of excitement persists throughout a career. More commonly, however, it eventually wears off. After a few months or a year at work, many people become a little depressed. They're still at the same desk, in the same cubicle, doing the same tasks.

The work may not be as fulfilling, and you're not even sure that it's being recognized. The daily grind of routine sets in, with a vacation break of just a few weeks on the distant horizon. The initial excitement begins to dissipate, and they're dying for a change.

As an international graduate working in your host country you might face additional burdens, such a requirements to keep your work visa. Demands may arise that you've avoided while a student, perhaps pressures from parents to get married or the need to pay back student loans. In addition, if you lived in a university dormitory while a student, you've now got to look after your own housing.

Feeling bored, or unfulfilled at work, or stressed about being in a new stage of your life are natural states of mind. Many corporations and large organizations are hierarchical. You may feel that you are at the bottom of a very long ladder. Everyone else is above you, and your behaviour is constantly under scrutiny.

Ironically, after years of dreaming about graduating and getting out, you might actually find that you miss being a student! At least university offered something new and different at the start of each semester or term – new courses, new classmates, new professors, and new assignments.

With graduation a new set of demands is placed on you, ones you've never had to consider before not only with regard to work, but from other facets of your life including family and friends. If you feel your life is not going as you envisioned it, remember that things are not as bad as they seem. Getting accustomed to the new rhythms of the workplace may take more than a year or even two. Making new friends at work will also take time.

If you miss university, you can always take a course. If it relates to your job, many employers will even pay part of your tuition. Alternatively, choose a subject that has nothing to do with work.

Most of all, don't limit your options in regard to work and beyond. Your university education as an international student gives you something special. The ultimate advantage of your university degree, especially as an international student, is flexibility.

Dealing with transition

Despite tests, exams, and assignments, many students become comfortable in the university environment. By the time they graduate, they will have figured out how school works. And if they're good students, they may also be having a lot of fun. As an international student, you also may have grown comfortable in your new environment.

Once you commence full-time post-university employment the rhythms and routines of school are different. At university, your work normally begins and ends within a few months, from the start of the semester to its conclusion. You advance in regular steps and get a degree in a relatively short time. At work, your career trajectory becomes far more elastic, with significant changes often taking much longer than you might expect.

It is an axiom that the workplace is characterized by change. But that won't necessarily apply to your personal advancement. In many cases you will eventually find your comfort zone at work.

However, if you find that you are very unhappy or impatient at work, the job is probably not right for you, and you need to move on. Don't look on this as something to be feared, but rather as a typical transition that most people undertake, likely more than once. Approach it as an opportunity for growth and renewed excitement.

If after a year, you decide that your job is not as rewarding as you'd expected, that is perfectly normal. After all, your first job is unlikely to match your ideal. Most people work two jobs during their first two years after graduation. Review Chapter 6 to evaluate your VIPS (values, interests, personality, and skills). These may have altered, as is normal. After all, a year or two into working full-time, you will not be the person you were in university.

Consult your network and learn about the jobs that are available to you that fit with your VIPS. Now you've got more skills and evidence of the kind of person you are in the workplace. This is especially the case for international students who are either working in a host country, or returned to their home country after studying abroad.

The transition from one job to another will be easier than the transition from school to work. In the two sections below, we discuss the strategies that any professional, at any stage of his or her career, needs to follow to effectively transition in the world of work.

Staying prepared

Once you start working full-time, your résumé becomes more important than ever. You will be surprised by how often you're asked for your résumé, sometimes at short notice. Update your résumé and LinkedIn profile every few weeks or months as you undertake new tasks and learn new skills. If you're continuing your education on a part-time basis, be sure to indicate this. Your language skills might also have improved.

Keep your list of references current as well. Your employer will be your key reference. For this reason, never burn your bridges at work, even if that means biting your tongue and swallowing your pride, difficult though it may be. Years later, you'll be glad you refrained from speaking your mind or acting impulsively, and may even recall difficult employers with fondness. In the same way, you may see your tough professors in a different light!

Keep up on your research in regard to the labour market. You will have developed your network while working and can start to touch base with key contacts. You may also find that you are being contacted by students graduating a year or two behind you as they prepare to search for their first job. Be generous in assisting them.

It is best to look for a job while still employed, so handing in your notice is usually not recommended until you have a firm offer. Of course, that depends on the job you have, and your specific circumstances.

Some jobs are so demanding in terms of time or pressure that you simply don't have the leisure to think, let alone engage in a job hunt. Some jobs don't provide you with the right contacts to build a decent network. These tend to be career dead ends. Bite the bullet: get out and begin a new job search.

If you do leave a position without a new one in hand, several months of hard work will probably elapse before you find a good job. Maintain your confidence during this time. When you doubt yourself, think of what you achieved by completing a university degree as an international student. If you could do that, you can do anything.

Try to avoid brooding on your situation. You won't feel unemployed if you treat your job search as full-time work. Get up early each day, dress as if you were going to the office, build your network, attend information interviews, rethink your career path, and assess your options.

Changing jobs is a transition that will certainly happen to you. Another transition that may be part of your life is going back to school.

Learning does not end

Learning will not end once you start work. Technology, laws, knowledge, and standards are continually changing and you need to stay abreast. On its own, the skill set developed at university will not see you very far along a career that will span decades.

After a year or more in the labour force, you'll have a more precise image of the ideal job. At that point, you may decide to go back to school and further your education. This may be part-time or perhaps full-time. In some cases your employer will expect or require that you complete a certification or other programme.

Many professional and graduate programmes at universities prefer applicants who have full-time work experience after earning their bachelor's degree. For some programmes, such as the MBA, having worked for several years is an entrance requirement.

The overriding focus of many professional and graduate programmes is to select applicants who have what it takes to finish the programme and make positive contributions to their professions. Although your past academic record matters when applying to university after having worked for a few years, so does what you've done in the workplace.

Many young people become international students after working for a year or two after completing their undergraduate education. This can be a brilliant strategy in many cases, as you've mastered the skills required to do well at school, and have a solid sense of your VIPS (values, interests, personality, and skills). If you look back to Figure 1.1 of Chapter 1, you will see that it is much more common for master's- and doctoral-level students to study internationally, than it is for bachelor-level students.

After completing my bachelor degree in economics in 2012 in Venezuela, I wanted to continue my studies and explored my options by attending different career fairs. I began to consider the pros and cons of studying abroad, such as leaving my family and friends behind, and studying in a different country in a different education system with a different culture.

Eventually, my option was clear: if I wanted to move and work outside my home, studying abroad would bring me more benefits. I started my MA in International Business in 2014 at Anglia Ruskin University in Cambridge in the United Kingdom and I was determined to do well as my final results would determine where I would go next. So I studied hard, engaged with the university by attending different seminars, special lectures, job fairs, and took part in the intern programmes of the business faculty.

This led me to find my first job, an internship at the European Bioinformatics Institute. This three-month internship eventually opened the opportunity of becoming a staff member as an event organizer. All this happened while I completed my MA in International Business, graduating with distinction and being the valedictorian of my class. I worked at the European Bioinformatics Institute for one and a half years until I moved on to a more promising position at the headquarters of the institute in Germany. My hard work and determination paid off: studying abroad really helped me to find a fantastic job and advance my career!

Maria Mercedes Bacadare Goitia

Further success

The road to the great job is just that: a road. You will encounter difficulties on the road, some possibly based on your gender, ethnic background, or personality. Again, the key is to trust your feelings and nourish your dreams.

As you progress in the world of work, you will acquire reliable colleagues and associates who will advise you. The support of your network will be critical to your success and happiness at work. One or more of your professors may well belong to it, as will some of your friends from university.

Regardless of where your path may lead, the advantages that you acquired as an international student will always be pertinent: problem-solving, good communication skills, strategic and creative thinking, adaptability, and the self-confidence that comes from your accomplishments. Use these well, and your ultimate success is assured.

Coping with mistakes

We all make mistakes. As an international student you've made your share as you adjusted to your new environment. As a newly hired employee and especially as an international graduate, you will make mistakes and do things you wished you had not. The key is not to avoid making mistakes, but rather how you respond.

If you screw up, take action right away. Suppose you sent an email or text that you soon regretted. The instinctive reaction is to wait and see, but this will compound the problem. Don't wait – apologize immediately to everyone who might be affected. Take ownership of the situation.

An email apology might read as follows:

> Dear Simone, I'm very sorry for the inappropriate message I sent you a few minutes ago. Please be assured that I did not intend to question your competency or your valuable contribution to the project. I am copying this email to all group members to inform them of my apology.

Apologies need not be long, but they must be sincere and timely. Apologize face to face as soon as you realize what you've done. This can just be a short sentence to the person you might have slighted. Don't transform the apology into an explanation: "I was tired and overloaded this morning. While trying to answer an urgent question from a supervisor, I sent the email without reading it carefully."

What people will remember is not your mistake, but rather how you dealt with the situation.

Social media and relationship building

Successful careers have always depended on networking and establishing positive relationships with others. Social media adds complexity to networking and relationship building.

Many careers and people have suffered, some horrendously so, because of the inappropriate use of social media. The daily news will tell you of numerous public stories. Just imagine how many similar stories occur that are not reported in the media.

Email, Facebook, Twitter, and other messaging services, platforms, and apps are pervasive in the workplace and essential for many tasks. The minute you send a message, you are engaging in a conversation with another person; in other words, you are entering into a relationship that could either help or hurt you in terms of what you want to do or where you want to go. Every single message is either a relationship builder or breaker.

All new employees, but especially internationally educated workers, must be hyper-sensitive to what is acceptable. Many unhappy scenarios begin with a simple email or text communication. Many positive relationships can develop if you treat email or texting as an engagement with other people.

A rude or ill-thought-out email message or text can be forwarded to anyone, anywhere, at any time, and it remains in a folder long after a spoken comment has been forgotten. Take extra time when sending a message, and remember that language that was acceptable as a student, may not be once you become an employee.

Consider the nature of all your written messages at work. Do they reflect positive, optimistic, organized, and energized qualities – the kind of qualities that people find appealing?

Branding yourself

Employers and recruiters increasingly investigate the online presence of potential employees, looking to find the ideal candidates. Some recruiters would rather visit a webpage than read a résumé or cover letter. Many people, including potential friends and colleagues, will turn to the internet to learn about you, or the learn more about you. This is particularly so as an internationally educated worker who may not have a long history of residence in a specific city or country.

In Chapter 6 we showed you how services like LinkedIn are critical in many countries for networking and job searching. In some professions, and in many jobs, your employer may post material about you online, such as your education, accomplishments, and expertise.

To use the language of business, everyone, whether he or she likes it, is a brand. If you have no online presence whatsoever, that is a negative brand. It communicates either that you have accomplished nothing, are technology incompetent, or are a hermit.

The image that you send (or don't send) into the world may not be the real or the complete you, but it is you as the world sees you. That's why you should be diligent in developing and promoting your online brand.

Now, this doesn't mean transforming yourself into a marketer. Rather, we encourage you to be proactive by constructing a virtual version of yourself that will help you achieve your goals at work and in life.

A simple way of doing this – beyond LinkedIn – is to establish your own website. A well-designed webpage, which is easily created from free software, helps you to control the messages that you send out. At the cost of a few hours, you'll have a site that potential employers and others can visit. You may well already have created a website as a university student.

The site can be the central location for information about you, including your résumé. You can link this to your LinkedIn page and other sites. You can post your school work (after all, it is your work), volunteer activities, and anything else that you've done: photos, art, travel, and more. This is also a way to inform others of your home country, culture, and background.

However, remember that everything you post must be carefully selected. It's your job to project and protect a positive self-image online. This means never putting silly or salacious images and comments on the internet, or using photos without permission of those in them.

The most critical piece of advice in creating your webpage is to keep everything upbeat, without looking like a naive optimist. You want to avoid negativity, even if you think it's clever, sophisticated, and urbane. A corollary of this is that, if you link to other websites, ensure that they too avoid negativity – you can always be damned by association.

A personal website is a powerful tool to introduce yourself to others. This can be especially helpful if you think that co-workers, clients, or others may have a mistaken perception of who you are. This often happens to international students and internationally educated workers, solely because those you interact with are not knowledgeable about your culture.

There are numerous apps that allow you to frame and manipulate multimedia materials in a creative and individualistic manner. In an internet universe, where any piece of music can be paired with any photo and both can be manipulated to achieve virtually any end, investing some creative energy in a website has a huge payoff.

When branding yourself, be aware of the way in which others might interpret you. Too many websites are egotistical exercises in self-discovery and self-promotion, which is the least effective kind of marketing.

If you use Twitter, Facebook, or similar platforms be certain that the privacy settings are such that your posts and photos are not in the public domain. You may wish to review the privacy options for the platforms and services you use, and conduct a web search with your name.

A final word

You are on an amazing journey. As an international student you've made your life so much remarkable than would otherwise have been the case. You've opened many doors, and closed some as well. You have expanded your knowledge and developed new skills while also enhancing your personal, social, and cultural strengths.

As the quotation at the start of this chapter emphasizes, you cannot travel back in time to change any aspect of the journey. However, you can decree how the journey goes from now on.

About the authors

Thomas R. Klassen is a Professor at York University in Toronto, Canada. He has taught in a variety of programmes, including the IMBA at the Schulich School of Business, the Department of Political Science, the School of Public Policy and Administration, and the Faculty of Health. He has taught university courses in South Korea (at Yonsei University) and Germany (at the University of Konstanz). He divides his time between Toronto (Canada) and Seoul (South Korea).

Dr Klassen has published widely including on how to ensure that university students succeed in their studies and employment. He is co-author of *How to Succeed at University (and Get a Great Job!): Mastering the Critical Skills You Need for School, Work and Life* (2015), which was published in French in 2018 as *Décrocher son diplôme universitaire (et l'emploi de vos rêves!): Comment maîtriser les compétences essentielles menant au succès à l'école, au travail et dans la vie*.

He is lead editor of *The Routledge Handbook of Global Public Policy and Administration* (2017). He is a sought-after international expert on workplace and labour market related topics. He holds a PhD in organizational behaviour.

Dr Klassen was born in São Paulo, Brazil, and lived there for a dozen years. His mother was born in Germany and his father in Russia. His spouse is from South Korea, and his 12-year-old twins have three passports each.

More information about him can be found at www.thomasklassen. net. He would be delighted to hear from you at tklassen@yorku.ca.

 **Christine Menges** is Director of the Career Center, MBA Programs, at the WHU-Otto Beisheim School of Management, one of Germany's top business schools according to major national and international rankings. She is passionate about helping others to learn and grow so they may realize their potential to achieve the goals and dreams they hold for themselves and for their organizations.

Dr Menges has crafted WHU's career counselling approach and placement strategy for students with work experience, including Kellogg-WHU Executive MBA students and WHU's full- and part-time MBA students. She forges networks with industry leaders in order to advise students in their career progression and transition to new employment opportunities. Dr Menges has presented her unique approach at major conferences and has held workshops with leading personnel companies.

She has over ten years of work experience in the higher education sector as a researcher, teacher, and department head at universities in Switzerland and the United Kingdom, and as a consultant and trainer for private and public organizations. She holds a PhD in management with a special focus on mentoring, from the University of St. Gallen in Switzerland. As an international student, she lived in countries in three continents – America, Asia, and Europe.

Rooted in the beautiful surroundings of Germany's most southern Alpine region, the Allgäu, she is a dedicated skier, mountain climber, and outdoor enthusiast. She shares the wonders of this world with her husband and her three children.

More information about Dr Menges is at www.christinemenges. de. You may reach her at info@christinemenges.de.

CPSIA information can be obtained
at www.ICGtesting.com
Printed in the USA
LVHW030021071219
639738LV00003B/136/P